# Crocodiles

# CROCODILES

*Their natural history, folklore and conservation*

C.^harles A. W. *Guggisberg*

*STACKPOLE BOOKS : HARRISBURG*

Published in USA by
STACKPOLE BOOKS
Cameron & Kelker Streets
Harrisburg, PA 17105

© C. A. W. Guggisberg  1972

Library of Congress Cataloging in Publication Data

Guggisberg, Charles Albert Walter.
    Crocodiles: their natural history, folklore
and conservation.

    Bibliography: p.
    1. Crocodiles. I. Title
QL666.C9G8    598.14    73-179600
ISBN 0-8117-0460-2

Printed in Great Britain

# Contents

# List of Illustrations

## Plates

## List of Illustrations

*Photographs not otherwise acknowledged are from the author's collection*

### Line drawings

### Maps

# Preface

THE crocodiles, alligators and caimans both horrify and fascinate observers; lurid travellers' tales of evil reptiles lying loglike in tropical mud, ready to snatch and devour the unwary human, linger in the memory. Even naturalists have dismissed this strange family as 'ugly murderous brutes', and the 'hate-the-croc' campaign has been fanned by a frantic commercial greed for their skins.

What truth lies in the stories of savage man-eating crocodiles? How do the saurians really live, how and where do they hunt, eat and breed? What is their ecological importance? What are their future prospects?

It is a story of endless interest. The crocodiles have an immensely long evolutionary history, dating back to mesozoic times, the days of the dinosaurs. For something like 140 million years they have remained the dominant predators of tropical, and some sub-tropical, lakes and rivers, as the great majority of reptiles became extinct, never being ousted by mammals or fish. They lay enough eggs for heavy losses in the early stages not to affect their numbers; they have long lives and few enemies once they reach maturity; they can even live in marginal areas where their prey is scarce for part of the year. They are comparatively widely distributed: America has alligators and caimans and no less than four species of crocodile, while crocodiles are also found in Africa, Australia, New Guinea and south-eastern Asia. Only in the last twenty-five years have they been seriously threatened—by man.

Their success story is evidence of their excellent adaptation to their amphibious existence; their anatomy and physiology have great interest. So do their relations with man, by whom they have been venerated, eaten and dreaded. Now, for the first time, they are slaughtered for shoes and handbags on a scale that is defeating even their resilience. The American alligator is on the list of 'animals in danger' compiled by the International Union for the Conservation of Nature, and in Australia, India, South America and elsewhere the threat looms large.

## Preface

The present author, a naturalist with a personal acquaintance with crocodiles that started with an expedition on the Victoria Nile described at the beginning of this book, is convinced that a wider knowledge of the life and habits of the crocodile family will show that the moves now afoot to protect them are not solely because their extermination has already been shown to upset the ecological balance in the areas concerned. As living monuments of almost unbelieveable antiquity, as tourist attractions for areas urgently needing trade, and simply for what they are, they deserve to survive.

Dr F. Vollmar,
*Secretary General
of the World Wildlife
Fund*

# 1 The River of Crocodiles

*A narrow escape: Charles Baldwin attacked by a crocodile* (Baldwin)

THERE was a period in the long history of our planet Earth when the reptiles were the masters of all creation. They dominated the land, the water and the air—and a fabulous spectacle they must have made, the dinosaurs and pterodactyls, the ichthyosaurs and plesiosaurs. Many a naturalist must have dreamed of having a time machine that would carry him back to mesozoic times and give him a glimpse of this reptilian era.

Sir Arthur Conan Doyle's vivid imagination conjured up a small remnant of the Mesozoic on a South American highland plateau, surrounded by dense, impenetrable forest, and he had his hero, Professor Challenger, lead an exploring expedition into this 'Lost World'. Naturalists and camera hunters are sure to deplore the fact that no real 'Lost World' with living dinosaurs has been discovered in any part of the world. At one time there were persistent rumours of a 'Brontosaurus' lurking in the vast marshes of Lake Bangweolo, but no evidence for the existence of such a creature has ever come to light, and it must be considered as having had no more reality than the much publicised 'Yeti' or the mammoths some explorers hoped to find roaming through the Siberian forests.

Although no dinosaur has survived into the Age of Man—contrary to what cartoonists would have us believe—there were, until a short time ago, a good number of 'Lost Worlds' where it was possible to see mesozoic reptilian life—tropical and subtropical rivers, lakes and marshes swarming with crocodiles, alligators and caimans, all of which must be considered as close cousins and contemporaries of the dinosaurs. William Bartram, the eighteenth-century naturalist, found such a 'Lost World' in Florida; more recent travellers filmed and photographed impressive mesozoic scenes on the island of Marajo, situated within the mouth of the mighty Amazon; and Sir Samuel Baker, the African explorer, came upon a reptilian dorado on his way up the Victoria Nile—one of the few that has not changed appreciably since it was first seen by European eyes.

The crocodilians survived when the dinosaurs faded out, and for untold millions of years they managed to remain the dominant predators of tropical rivers and lakes. Most authors dismissed them summarily as 'ugly, murderous brutes', but as a naturalist I wanted to learn more about these mesozoic relics, to find out something about their habits. In 1952 I had a first opportunity to get personally acquainted with the big reptiles, when my wife and I teamed up with Wally and Dick, two American cameramen, in organising an expedition to Sir Samuel Baker's 'Lost World'. The now famous Murchison Falls National Park was at that time a mere game reserve, and nobody had yet thought of building a safari lodge on the banks of the Victoria Nile. It had been our intention to do a bit of bush-bashing and to drive our two jeeps to the Murchison Falls across trackless country, but the game warden of the area advised against this and lent us the Game Department launch with her crew of two. After leaving the port of Butiaba we chugged over Lake Albert for three hours with not much to see except for an occasional tern and two or three pelicans. Floating papyrus islands began to appear, just a few at first, then more and more, and in places the surface of the lake began to be covered with the light green rosettes of the plant known as Nile cabbage. The crews of a dozen dugouts were busy hauling in nets: judging from the numerous silvery flashes the catch was a good one, and having ordered the helmsman-cum-engineer to heave to, we took movie shots and photographs of the fishermen and bought a dozen fish as an addition to our provisions.

On we went, threading our way between innumerable floating islands, which began to crowd in until we found ourselves between two unbroken walls of papyrus. We had entered one of the arms of the Victoria Nile, and from the cabin roof we looked out across a vast expanse of swampland, its dark green enlivened by the white wings of numerous egrets. Pied kingfishers hovered over the open water, diving for fish at frequent intervals, and a goliath heron stood motionless on a floating island that came drifting slowly towards the launch. There was a sudden swirl of water on the edge of the papyrus—but we could not see whether it was caused by a big fish or a crocodile. Often it looked as if we were in a blind alley, but the helmsman knew his way about this watery maze, for whenever we thought that this time we surely would have to turn back, a new stretch of navigable water opened up ahead.

Some trees peeping over the tufted papyrus tops indicated that dry land was not far away, and we finally emerged from the swampy channel into the actual river, giving a fright to two hippos which, at our sudden appearance, crash-dived with angry snorts. Shortly afterwards the first crocodile slithered into the water.

Before long four or five of the big reptiles were spotted lying on the low river bank. The helmsman had hardly altered course when the nearest crocodile jerked its body up on to the full height of its short legs and ran towards the water. Before it had yet plunged into the river, the others were moving too, and they all disappeared long before we had a chance to take any pictures. This happened again and again, the saurians turning out to be much more timid and wary than we had expected.

The ground on both sides of the river rose rapidly, and soon we were in a broad but steep-sided valley. The glassy surface of the slow-flowing Nile faithfully mirrored every little detail of the lofty

*Crocodiles running down the river bank*

palms and picturesque groups of trees fringing its banks. Our navigator now steered towards one of these clumps of trees, and the other crewman, who stood at the bow and acted as pilot, extended his arm. 'Mamba,—mamba mingi sana—crocodiles, lots of crocodiles!'

In the shade of the trees lay thirty or forty crocodiles, closely packed, scaly back beside scaly back, most of them with open mouth, displaying rows of pointed teeth. As we approached, movie camera in position, some began to move and a dozen bodies slid down into the river. There were still enough crocodiles on land, however, to satisfy the most exacting photographer.

The helmsman cut the engine, and the launch went gliding on noiselessly, with gradually diminishing speed. Another crocodile rushed down the bank, then two, and finally the whole mass of them came alive. For a few moments there was a tremendous commotion as a couple of dozen dragons began pushing and heaving, almost crawling over each others' backs. The bank was fairly steep, and they did not run, but came tobogganing down on their bellies, the water boiling and seething under the impact of their bodies. It was a fascinating spectacle, a primeval scene out of a long-past age. We felt sorry when it was over and the saurians had all gone.

All? No, one huge crocodile, remarkable not only for its length, but also for its enormous girth and bulk, still lay underneath the drooping branches. The launch slowly drifted against the bank and came to a halt close to the somnolent monster. While our cameras clicked and whirred, the helmsman said that he knew this 'mamba' well and had often seen it in exactly the same place. 'Mzee kabisa—very old'.

Deep in its mesozoic dreams, the crocodile went on sleeping, apparently unaware that it was being filmed from a distance of a few metres only. As we wanted pictures showing it in motion, we yelled and waved our hats, but only when the pilot jumped ashore and approached it with a long pole, did this grandfather of all crocodiles suddenly wake up. It came lumbering down the incline and threw itself into the river, almost colliding with the launch. Foam shot up, the water splashed over the immensely broad armour-plated back, formed an eddying whirlpool, and then became as smooth and oily again as if nothing had happened. From then on we ignored the innumerable crocodiles which were lying on the banks singly or in small groups and left proceedings in the hands of the helmsman, who knew all the places they especially favoured; our cameras reaped rewarding harvest.

*Crocodiles on the Victoria Nile*

The frequent changes of scenery alone would have made this first river trip an unforgettable experience. The long stretches of dense gallery forest, festooned all over with lianas, were from time to time broken by steep cliffs, where trees tottered in a precarious balance, with most of their roots hanging free, ready to tumble into the river during the next rains. Beyond the forest belt we could see the bush-covered sides of the gradually narrowing valley. Sometimes there were marshy reed beds, 100 metres or more across, between the bank and the navigable part of the river, then again we chugged along practically underneath the spreading branches of mighty kigelia trees whose fruit

looked like monstrous sausages suspended on strings. We caught
glimpses of darkly mysterious backwaters, and of deep bays framed
by a lush profusion of tropical vegetation.

On the mudflats and sandbanks, there were groups of hippos, a
dozen here, two dozen there, and once a herd of about 100. As the
boat was steered as close to them as the shallow water would permit, a
ponderous stampede was started; snorting and grunting, throwing up
tremendous bow waves, the huge creatures made for a deeper part of
the river, a few pairs of ears becoming all that could be seen above
water. We saw small troops of waterbuck and large herds of Uganda
kob. A bull buffalo, which had just been drinking, raised its magnifi-
cently horned head and eyed the approaching launch suspiciously
before turning round and storming up the bank. Baboons disported
themselves on the cliffs, and on a shallow backwater, too far away for
our cameras, we spotted three black rhinoceroses, probably a bull,
a cow and a nearly full grown youngster.

Some elephants moving parallel to the river about halfway up the
bushy hillside looked as if they might eventually come to the water,
but after half an hour or so they gradually disappeared in the shady
depth of a patch of forest, leaving only an occasional flapping ear to be
seen. In a patch of thornbushes covering an island in midstream we
discovered a breeding colony of darters. It was possible to get so close
that the bow of the launch slid right underneath the branches, and
from the roof of the cabin we could look into the nests, flattish platforms
built of twigs and much exposed to the sun. The young birds seemed
to suffer from the midday heat, for their white distended throats were
in continuous vibrating movement. The adults paid little attention to
the boat, only the owners of the few nearest nests staying away.

Bird life on the Victoria Nile was both plentiful and varied, though
the constant preoccupation with crocodiles, hippos and elephants left
too little time for ornithological observations. Fish eagles sat on the
kigelia trees, hadadas uttered their loud and discordant calls, hammerkops flapped along the river bank with owl-like wing-beats. On the
sandbanks and mudflats were big flocks of tree ducks, Egyptian geese
and spurwing geese, with common sandpipers running around among
the bigger birds. Wherever the banks were swampy, innumerable
lily-trotters and stilts could be seen, as well as flocks of cattle egrets,
good numbers of blackheaded herons and the occasional goliath

heron. Spurwinged plovers and water dikkops were specially common on the hauling-out places of the crocodiles.

The current became stronger the farther we ascended. White foam began to appear in patches and long bands, as if a giant were doing his washing somewhere upriver. A few elephants stood on a swampy meadow. Two hills rose up in front of us, jutting out into the valley from both sides and reducing the width of the foam-covered river. They formed something like a gate, through which we could look into a narrow gorge-like valley, ending, so it seemed, in a dark towering cliff. But no—there was a deep cleft in this rocky wall, a cleft out of which rose clouds of steamy-looking spray—the spray of the Murchison Falls. Now we knew the source of the foam that drifted for so many kilometres downriver.

For just a moment we saw the falls in their full grandeur, but as the launch turned towards the left bank, the two hills seemed to move together, shutting out the stupendous view and closing the gorge to our eyes as if the gigantic gate had suddenly been locked. A couple of minutes later the boat lay tied up at the small pier that still carried the name of Fajao, a government station which had been given up many years ago at the time when sleeping-sickness had swept through this part of Uganda, killing thousands of people and causing vast stretches of land to revert to wilderness. We had reached our camping site.

A tent for the Americans was pitched underneath a huge tree. As it was a beautifully clear evening, Rosanne and I slept in the open, on the pier. The fish we had bought before leaving Lake Albert were too bony to make a satisfactory meal. The natives had called them 'ngara', and we identified them as a species of Alestes, probably *Alestes baremose:* I cannot recommend it as a food fish!

I lay awake, looking up at the twinkling stars, listening to the noises of the night—the calls of water dikkops, heard above the continuous basso grunts of the hippos, and a lot of splashing and spattering in midstream could be heard. Some of this could be caused by jumping fish, but I became convinced that it was mainly due to the activities of crocodiles. Were they chasing each other? Or chasing after fish? An elephant trumpeted somewhere downstream—and I fell asleep.

A long walk next morning to see the Murchison Falls, where the mighty Victoria Nile forces its way through a crack about 6 metres in width, forms no part of this story. We did, however, see a big concentration of crocodiles on a small island some way below the falls. Later, rowing to the other side of the river from our camp, we were forced by a couple of dozen hippos disporting themselves in midstream to make a long detour upriver, but this enabled us afterwards to drift silently and without unnecessary movements along the outer side of a spit of land which tailed out in a series of bushy islands. Coming on to them in this way, we got fairly close to some of the crocodiles I had glimpsed from the camp, but they were still amazingly shy. A flock of tree ducks had not shown any signs of taking wing when the last saurian had already plunged into the river. Rounding the end of the spit and entering a quiet backwater, up to about 100 scaly backs could be seen, the greatest number I have ever seen at one time. As we penetrated their refuge, one after the other sank out of sight, and a pattern of shiny lines radiated away from us as they cautiously went off, swimming close beneath the surface.

'Kenge', said my companion and pointed towards a tree leaning far out over the water. I made out a Nile monitor stretched out on the trunk; a few strokes of the oars moved the dinghy in the direction of the big lizard, which slid down the tree and vanished among the bushes at its base just before we came within photographic range.

Among the islands that formed something like a prolongation of the spit, luck favoured us at once. A big crocodile came lumbering through the high marsh grass surrounding the island, and lay for a moment practically alongside the dinghy, offering a chance for a splendid close-up before it moved into deeper water, pushing itself forward with undulating movements of its formidable tail. Then the crewman forced the dinghy into the grass and jumped ashore, waving to me to follow. We had not penetrated far into the thicket covering the island when a slithering noise and a splash here, a crack and a rumble there, made me realise that we had literally walked into a concentration of crocodiles, all of which were now beating a very hasty retreat. The air was impregnated with their musky smell, and the ground beneath the bushes looked churned up, as if somebody had been digging for buried treasure. Fragments of crocodiles' eggs lay about in great abundance and indicated that we had come upon a favourite breeding ground.

The crewman spotted a young crocodile, not over 70 cm in length,

*Nile crocodile*

but our attempts to corner the little animal were in vain; it wriggled
through the bushes with great agility and managed to make good its
escape. I broke off a branch and started poking about in the sand
without, however, finding any eggs. The month was September, and
I did not then know that the crocodiles of the lower Victoria Nile lay
their eggs in December and during the first half of January. As the
crocodiles were now thoroughly disturbed, we headed back towards
Fajao Pier; Wally had been fishing, catching not only several 'ngara',
but also a good-sized catfish, which provided a fine supper. As the sun
disappeared behind the horizon, I climbed on to the cabin roof and sat
a while watching the river. There were no more crocodiles on land,
but a considerable amount of movement in the water; despite the
rapidly fading light numbers of them could be seen swimming to and
fro. Occasionally one would lift its head above the water and make

champing movements with its jaws: presumably a fish was being killed and juggled into a proper position for swallowing.

Next morning, crossing again to the right bank, and taking cover among some rocks overlooking the spit, my thoughts went back for almost ninety years, to 1863, and to the first Europeans to come up the Victoria Nile. After having discovered Lake Albert, Samuel White Baker—soon to become Sir Samuel Baker—and his courageous wife wanted to make sure that the river they had seen in Kamrasi's country and knew, from Speke's account, to be coming out of Lake Victoria, really did flow into their new lake. They found the mouth of the Victoria Nile without any difficulty and followed its course until further progress by canoe was barred by the falls, which Baker named after Sir Roderick Murchison, President of the Royal Geographical Society. I was amazed to see how little this area had changed in almost a century. Apart from Fajao Pier and the launch, the Bakers, could they have come up the river again, would have noticed no signs of civilisation whatever, and the congregation of crocodiles at the various basking places would have been entirely familiar. 'I never saw such an extraordinary show of crocodiles as were exposed on every sandbank on the sides of the river', Baker wrote in his fascinating book *The Albert Nyanza*, which makes as good reading today as when it was first published. 'They lay like logs of timber close together, and upon one bank we counted twenty-seven, of large size; every basking place was crowded in a similar manner.' As the explorers approached the falls, they saw still more crocodiles. 'There was a sandbank on our left, which was literally covered with crocodiles lying parallel to each other like trunks of trees prepared for shipment; they had no fear of the canoe until we approached within about twenty yards of them, when they slowly crept into the water. All excepting one, an immense fellow who lazily lagged behind.'

In Baker's time the country round about was inhabited, with fishermen's huts on the banks of the river. The crocodiles were, therefore, used to canoes and showed less fear of man than they did ninety years later.

My musings were brought to a sudden end when, after waiting only about twenty minutes, I heard a sudden 'pat-pat-pat' on wet mud and saw a crocodile walk up from the water to settle down fairly close to the foot of the hill on which I sat. It was almost immediately followed by another, and before an hour had gone by well over twenty had hauled out on the spit, most of them about 30 metres from my hiding place. I had many good shots—not with the 'trusty Fletcher', as Baker used to call his favourite gun, but with my equally trusty Leica. Next day I cut some branches and stuck them into the soil among the bushes fringing the edge of the backwater, thus constructing what I considered a fairly dense screen of leaves. Behind this 'scherm', as the old South African hunters used to say, I sat, considerably nearer to the place where the majority of the crocodiles had basked in the sun.

There is, however, no doubt that they saw right through my camouflage: not a single one came to the spit. Then, after a lengthy wait, I suddenly became aware that three were gradually drifting nearer and nearer to the place where I crouched behind that inadequate screen. Showing only the eyes, a few square centimetres of scaly skin between them, and at intervals the nostrils, they came infinitely slowly inching forward. I cannot say that I saw them 'move', but whenever I had looked away and then turned back to them, I found that they were somewhat closer. Thus they literally stalked me, and then kept watching me intently from a distance of about 3 or 4 metres. I was probably quite safe on dry land, but it gave me a decidedly eerie feeling to have these three reptiles waiting patiently for me to oblige them by putting a foot into the water. They certainly gave an excellent demonstration of how they manage to get within striking distance of animals coming to drink from the river. We stared at each other for a couple of hours, in fact, until a short but heavy shower forced me to leave my post and to take shelter under some big trees on the nearby hillside.

The crocodiles seen at Fajao spent the daylight hours very lazily, leaving the water quite early in the morning to doze on the various basking places. Later, when the sun began to beat down hotly, many of them moved into the shade of trees or bushes, while others withdrew into shallow water where their bodies were only partly exposed to the scorching rays. They might take prey at any time, if conditions happened to be favourable—the three crocodiles stalking me in midday gave ample proof of this—but their period of greatest activity was definitely at dusk and during the night. Obviously fish must form an important part of their diet, much more important than I had

*A hauling-out site at Fajao*

hitherto imagined. Enormous numbers of fish were being destroyed here, hour after hour, day after day; there was, of course, no way of assessing the crocodiles' part in this perpetual slaughter, for they were by no means alone—there could be no doubts about the big quantities of fish eaten by the numerous cormorants, darters, herons, fish eagles, and kingfishers. In spite of all this, the river was swarming with fish, and Wally found himself in a real angler's paradise; he caught a lot more than our party could possibly eat. Fishermen in Europe have long been hurling accusations at otters, kingfishers, grey herons, and crested grebes, wanting them eradicated as vermin of the worst kind, but if the fish are rapidly disappearing from rivers and lakes, this is due to overfishing and even more to catastrophic water pollution. The fault lies with the humans and not with the birds and mammals feeding on fish. Co-existing with so-called 'vermin', the European fish populations have been flourishing for thousands of years—only to be brought to the verge of destruction by modern man!

On this first visit to the River of Crocodiles we must have seen well over 1,000 of these fascinating animals. Since then, we have been back many times, but we have never again seen them in quite such numbers. Even though the area was declared a national park some time after the memorable trip described above, poachers have been very busy, specially on the lower reaches of the river. Yet the Victoria Nile below the Murchison Falls still contains what is today one of the largest concentrations of crocodiles in all Africa. At the moment it even looks as if the park authorities have at last won the upper hand. Poachers have been operating on a smaller scale, and the badly depleted crocodile population at Magungo in the lower part of the river is building up again. On a recent aerial reconnaissance about 600 basking crocodiles were counted from Lake Albert to the Murchison Falls.

Though you may not yet see as many crocodiles as we did in 1952, you will be able to photograph them much more easily. They have become used to motor launches, just as they were used to the canoes in Baker's time, and it is possible to get excellent close-ups where on our first trip most of them hastily plunged into the river when the launch was still about 30 metres away.

The river scenery, too, is not quite the same as it was then. The floods of 1962 altered the aspect of the Falls and brought about many other changes. Fajao Pier has gone, and so has the spit of land which I found such an excellent place for watching and photographing crocodiles.

# 2. Crocodiles, Alligators, Caimans and Gavials

*Black caimans* (Brehm: Tierleben)

THE reptilian Order of *Crocodilia* consists of the following families: *Crocodylidae*, with the genera *Crocodylus, Osteolaemus* and *Tomistoma;* *Alligatoridae*, with the genera *Alligator, Caiman, Melanosuchus*, and *Palaeosuchus;* and *Gavialidae*, with the genus *Gavialis*. This enumeration will probably bring forth the inevitable question: what difference is there between crocodiles and alligators?

In crocodiles the teeth of the upper and lower jaws are more or less in line and, therefore, all well visible when the jaws are closed, which gives a crocodile that well-known grinning expression. The fourth tooth of the lower jaw, which is considerably longer than its neigh-

*Nile crocodile: the fourth tooth of the lower jaw is considerably longer than its neighbour and fits into a constriction of the snout*

*Alligator: the lower teeth are inside the upper row and the fourth tooth fits into a pit in the upper jaw*

bours, fits into a constriction of the snout and can be seen pointing upwards almost like a tusk. Alligators and caimans have the lower teeth inside the upper row and the enlarged fourth tooth fits into a pit in the upper jaw, thus becoming invisible. In very old individuals it occasionally grows to such a length that it pierces the upper jaw and sticks out on top.

Crocodiles are found not only in Africa, south-eastern Asia, New Guinea and Australia, but also in parts of America. Alligators and caimans are restricted to America, with the exception of one species of alligator which occurs in a small part of Asia.

The name 'alligator', which originated from the Spanish 'el lagarto' for 'the lizard', is frequently applied to crocodiles. Such a good field-naturalist as David Livingstone, for instance, almost constantly referred to the crocodiles he encountered in his African travels as 'alligators'. In Liberia and Ghana, the Nile crocodile is generally known as 'alligator', while the Australians have the habit of calling the big estuarine crocodile 'alligator', reserving the designation 'crocodile' for the smaller Australian freshwater crocodile. Australia has an Alligator River, Alligator Creek, Alligator Swamp, Alligator Lagoon—but no alligators.

Some last-century authors used 'alligators' as a collective name for the various South American caimans, even though recognising them as specifically different from the North American alligator. With the caimans belonging to the alligator-family, this can be considered as permissible. The name 'caiman', which comes from the Carib word 'acayoman', is, however, commonly applied to crocodiles in the French-speaking countries of West Africa and in Madagascar, having presumably got there from French Guyana.

'Gavial' owes its existence to an erroneous spelling of the Hindustani name 'gharial' for the long-snouted fish-eating crocodile, and quite a number of authors prefer the use of 'gharial' to 'gavial'. As the latter spelling has become firmly established in several languages and is also perpetuated in the generic name 'Gavialis'—which, according to the rules of nomenclature, cannot be changed—it might be just as well to drop the etymologically correct 'gharial'.

The derivation of 'crocodile' is similar, though much more ancient than that of 'alligator'. Writing about the crocodile of Egypt, Herodotus tells us: 'The name of this animal is not "krokodeilos", but "champsai". The Ionians call it "krokodeilos", because it reminds them of the "krokodeilos"—lizards—living on the stone walls of their homeland'. The agile little wall lizard, *Lacerta muraria*, of the Greek villages has thus given its name to the big saurian of the Nile.

The Nile crocodile, *Crocodylus niloticus*, was, of course, the first crocodilian to become known to Europeans, and even today it is for most people 'the crocodile'. The close links that existed between ancient Greece and Egypt brought the big reptile to the notice of Greek travellers at a very early date, and Herodotus published his famous account of its appearance and habits in the fifth century BC. He was, of course, not in a position to verify all the various bits of information he picked up, and what he finally offered to the public could not be anything but a mixture of fact and fable. His writings on the subject were, however, extensively quoted by Aristotle, who apparently never had a chance of seeing a live crocodile, and by many subsequent writers. We shall see that the part of his story which was dismissed with the greatest scorn by many modern authors has eventually been proved to be perfectly true.

In 58 BC the Aedile Scaurus brought to Rome not only the first hippopotamus ever seen in the Western World, but also the first crocodiles of which we have a record. It seems strange that Julius Caesar, returning from Egypt with a giraffe in 46 BC, should not also have had a few crocodiles among his luggage, but, if he did, nobody bothered to mention them. Egypt now being a part of the Roman Empire, it soon became known that the inhabitants of Tentyra, or Dendera, made quite a speciality of catching the scaly monsters. In 2 BC some Tentyrites were taken to Rome, together with thirty-six crocodiles, and a pool was dug in the Circus Flaminius so that they could demonstrate their far-famed skill in roping the reptiles.

Elagabalus, who ruled from AD 218 to 222 and made himself famous by driving lions in harness, is known to have had some crocodiles in his menagerie of mainly African animals. When it fell to the consul Quintus Aurelius Symmachus to organise the Praetorian Games of AD 400, he began to make arrangements for collecting animals three years ahead of the date. He obtained a number of crocodiles and gave orders for them to be kept alive after the first games, as he was keen to show them to a relative absent from Rome at the time. They apparently refused all food for fifty days, and most of them were killed in the 'ludi secundi' (second games), only two surviving the slaughter.

Symmachus was the last Roman consul to uphold pagan beliefs against Christianity, which had become the official religion under Constantine early in the fourth century. Christianity was soon to make Europeans acquainted with a literary reference to crocodiles, even though it took them a long time to realise its significance. When churchmen began browsing through the old Hebrew writings they came across a creature named Leviathan.

'Canst thou draw out Leviathan with an hook', Jehovah was supposed to have said to Job. 'Canst thou fill his skin with barbed irons? Or his head with fish spears? Who can open the doors of his face? His teeth are terrible round about. His scales are his pride, shut up together as with a close seal. In his neck remains strength . . .'

Generations of scholars must have wondered what frightful monster the Book of Job was referring to. It does, in fact, give quite a reasonable description of the crocodile, with which the Hebrews were well acquainted. Not only had they seen it in Egypt, but it also appeared in Palestine itself.

Well might the old Hebrews say: 'His teeth are terrible round about', for the full complement of the Nile crocodile's dentition is sixty-six. The snout is of medium length, triangular and moderately pointed. In young and very old specimens it forms an almost equilateral triangle. There are no ridges of any kind on forehead and muzzle.

Coming to 'Leviathan's' scales—'his pride' according to the Hebrews—we find a row of four keeled shields close behind the head, followed posteriorly by two small roundish scales, and six large keeled nuchal shields, arranged in two groups, one of four and one of two. In its broadest part the 'dorsal sheet' consists of eight rows of keeled shields.

The coloration is dark bronze above, with black spots on the back, and dirty yellow on the belly. The flanks are yellowish green with dark patches usually arranged in oblique stripes. There is, however, considerable variation, individuals from swift flowing rivers and from the vicinity of rapids often being lighter in hue than those living in lakes. The inside of the mouth can have a rather sickly yellow tinge, but it is more often deep orange, surprisingly vivid and producing a really beautiful splash of colour when the animal lies with its jaws wide open. Grotesque as this comparison may appear, a crocodile's jaw seen from afar always strikes me as reminiscent of a nestling bird's gape! The eyes are green.

The 'official' length of the Nile crocodile ranges from 3.80 to 5 metres. Reports of anything over 5 metres are apt to cause raised eyebrows among herpetologists, and the person publishing such measurements will find himself suspected of gross exaggeration. Herpetologists cannot be blamed for their sceptical attitude, for it is extremely easy to overestimate the length of a crocodile. I had a very salutary demonstration of this on my very first trip up the Victoria Nile. The sluggish monster which only moved into the water when one of our crewmen jumped ashore looked truly gigantic—at least 6 metres—when peered at through a camera's viewfinder. When it rushed down the bank, almost colliding with the bow of the launch, its length could be compared with that of the boat; paced off on the deck, it could certainly not have been longer than 5 metres—probably something between 4.50 and 5 metres. Shocked at my misjudgement, I subsequently paid close attention to the question of size, and on this and all later trips on the Victoria Nile I have never seen a crocodile of over 5 metres, and only very few approaching that length.

My crocodile hunting has all been done with a camera, and I am, therefore, unable to produce any measurements taken by myself, but searching through the available literature in order to find out what sizes crocodiles may reach, one finds a highly appropriate remark in Sir Harry Johnston's encyclopaedic work, *The Uganda Protectorate*. 'These creatures, as they lie on the rocks and sand, appear to be of enormous size and length, but actual measurements are apt to show that these estimates by eye are untrustworthy.' (How right he was.) Sir Harry Johnston never measured a crocodile of over 3.60 metres, but had reliable reports of 4.57 metre specimens. Cherry Kearton, the famous animal photographer, once watched an enormous crocodile crawl up on to a sandbank of the Semliki River. It was so much bigger than all the crocodiles already basking there that he thought it to measure about 27 ft—over 8 metres—in length. His companion, James Barnes, afterwards wrote: 'As far as could be judged by comparing his measurements with objects nearby, he was close to thirty feet in length. For the sake of natural science I would like to have applied a tape to his proportions'. Kearton and Barnes did not shoot the monster, and we shall never know how big it really was. On the photograph published in their book it certainly does look huge beside the other crocodiles—but how long were they?

Colonel J. Stevenson-Hamilton, for many years Warden of the Kruger National Park, recounts estimating a crocodile to be 5.50 metres long. He shot the animal and found the actual length to be 4.26 metres! For the crocodiles of the Kruger National Park, Stevenson-Hamilton gives an average of 3.65 metres. An acquaintance of mine who shot a good number of crocodiles in Tanganyika recorded the measurements of his four biggest as 4.09, 3.59, 3.25 and 3.12 metres.

R. C. F. Maugham, with considerable hunting experience in Mozambique, gave the length of his biggest crocodile as 17 ft—5.18 metres—with a girth of 7 ft 2 in. 'This, however, was an exceptionally large specimen,' he wrote, 'and was killed by me on the banks of the

Urema River in Cheringoma in 1904 and was, I suppose, quite 8 feet longer than the average length to which they attain in this part of Africa.' T. Murray Smith, a past president of the East African Professional Hunters' Association, recorded the length of a crocodile shot on Lake Tanganyika as 5.50 metres. It had a girth of 2.28 metres, the jaws were 71 cm across at the base, and the foreleg measured 56 cm. C. W. Hobley, known equally well as naturalist, anthropologist and colonial administrator, obtained a crocodile of 5.64 metres in the Miriu River.

Sir Samuel Baker never measured a specimen of over 18 ft—5.48 metres—but he felt sure that there existed crocodiles of over 6 metres. Near the Karuma Falls of the Victoria Nile he once caught sight of what looked like two enormous boulders on a low granite island. As the canoe approached, the boulders came to life and revealed themselves as two monster crocodiles, as thick as the body of a hippopotamus and with tremendously broad backs. Baker could not shoot, for there were hostile natives in the vicinity, and he did not want the noise of a firearm to attract their attention. 'I could not presume to estimate the length of these extraordinary creatures,' he later wrote.

Below the Murchison Falls, C. R. S. Pitman, who as game warden of Uganda came to know crocodiles very well indeed, had an encounter similar to that described by Sir Samuel Baker. 'Just ahead of me emerged the most appalling monstrosity I have ever seen,' he tells us, 'making slowly and laboriously for the water. It was a crocodile so old and bulky that it could only drag itself along on the ground with difficulty.' Pitman estimated the width across the back to be at least 1.50 metres, and was able afterwards to verify this by measuring the impression of the body and the distance between the footprints in the damp sand. He twice went back to look for this monster, which he found to be well known to the local natives, but he never saw it again. He believed that crocodiles could reach a length of 5.50 metres, perhaps occasionally 6.10.

In 1949, Erich Novotny, a professional hunter in Tanganyika, shot a 6.40 metre crocodile in the Emin Pasha Gulf of Lake Victoria, and he saw one in the same area which, by comparison with his canoe, seemed to have a length of 6.70 metres. According to Novotny, African fishermen of the Emin Pasha Gulf at that time quite frequently caught 6.10 and 6.70 metre crocodiles. Before World War I a crocodile of 6.60 metres was shot by the Duke of Mecklenburg at Mwanza, about 110 km east of Emin Pasha Gulf. The Juba River of Somalia used to have quite a reputation for big crocodiles, and Douglas Jones reported having measured one of 6.40 metres.

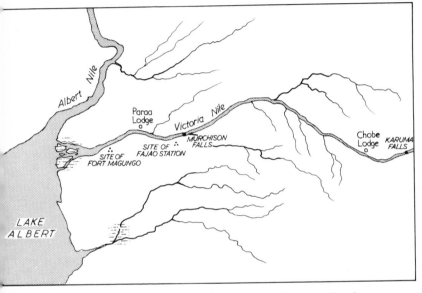

*Victoria Nile where it flows through Murchison Falls National Park*

The biggest crocodile measured by Mary Kingsley in West Africa had a length of 22 ft 3 in—6.77 metres— and the intrepid Victorian lady explorer added the following caustic commentary: 'Stay-at-home people will always discredit great measurements, but experienced bushmen do not, and after all, if it amuses the stay-at-homes to do so, by all means let them. They have dull lives of it and it does not harm you'. The measurement that comes nearest to Cherry Kearton's estimate of the Semliki River monster is a crocodile shot in Lake Kioga by Captain Riddick in 1916: it was 7.93 metres in length. A similar giant is recorded by Hans Besser, an excellent field naturalist whose reliability cannot be questioned; he shot it in 1903 on the Mbaka River, which enters Lake Nyasa from the Livingstone Mountains. At first sight he mistook the reptile for a big canoe half drawn up on the river bank, and after having secured it he found it to be

7.60 metres long, despite the fact that part of its tail was missing. The body was 93 cm high and had a girth of 4.26 metres. The skull was 1.40 metres in length and had a breadth of 93 cm. The five rivers flowing into Lake Nyasa from what was then German East Africa were at that time teeming with fish, and Besser noticed big crocodiles in all of them.

A. St H. Gibbons, who explored Barotseland and crossed Africa from south to north shortly after E. S. Grogan, considered the crocodiles of the Nile as being of a larger average size than those he had seen in the Zambezi. Erich Novotny, already mentioned in connection with the giant crocodiles of Emin Pasha Gulf, pointed out that of over 1,000 killed in the Malagarasy Swamp, the largest was only 3.65 metres in length. Hobley never obtained a crocodile of over 9 ft—2.74 metres—in Lake Baringo.

Some years before World War II the Aswa or Moroto River of northern Uganda became famous for its 'pygmy crocodiles', a mere 1.50 to 1.80 metres in length. They were first thought to represent a separate species, but when E. Temple-Perkins sent two specimens to London, the British Museum authorities declared them as absolutely identical with the Nile crocodile. Some habitats thus produce individuals of a fairly low average length, while others allow them to attain considerable dimensions. It takes a very long time for one of these saurians to grow to a length of 5 metres and over and we can safely assume that real giants have always been rare. None may now be surviving, after the slaughter of the last twenty-five years, in which the biggest specimens were the first to be killed off by professional hunters and poachers.

It must be mentioned that the textbooks permit the crocodiles of Madagascar to attain a length of 8 to 10 metres, this concession being based on some subfossil skeletal remains which A. Grandidier, the French naturalist, found in the Ambolisartra deposits. As the crocodiles of Madagascar had already been named *Crocodylus madagascariensis*, a new species, the Giant Crocodile, *Crocodylus robustus*, was described, but no live specimens have ever been obtained. If the name *robustus* is to be retained at all, it must be taken as referring to a crocodile that has been extinct for a considerable time. We now know that the living crocodiles of Madagascar, which according to Raymond Decary exceptionally attain a length of 6 metres, are identical with the Nile crocodile, and the specific name *madagascarensis* has been dropped long ago.

Hans Besser did not venture a guess as to the possible weight of his monster crocodile, but a 5.18 metre—17 ft—crocodile shot in the Kafue River has been recorded as weighing between 680 and 725 kg— 1,500 to 1,600 lb. George Cansdale very rightly remarks:

> It is almost impossible to estimate the weight of really large crocodiles, even when they have been killed. They cannot be loaded on a lorry and taken to a weighbridge; the only alternative is to cut them up and weigh them in pieces that can be lifted, as is done in the case of game animals, but for a large crocodile this would hardly be possible. An old Nile Crocodile, 14 feet in length and 7 feet in girth, was estimated at 2 tons; in other words, it must have had a volume of about 70 cubic feet.

In ancient times, crocodiles occurred in the delta of the Nile, the Pelusian arm of which reached the sea east of the present-day city of Port Said. It may have been from that point that the reptiles spread along the Mediterranean coastline and established themselves in the Nahr es Zerka, the only Palestinian river offering them a suitable habitat. Herodotus recorded the presence of crocodiles in Lake Moeris, which at that time filled up part of the Fayum depression.

C. S. Sonnini, the French naturalist who explored Egypt from 1777 to 1780, reported the saurians as 'banished' to the most southern parts of the country. Ascending the Nile he saw his first specimen between the villages of Sahet and Farshut, about halfway from Girga to Dendera. Sonnini found the animals to be very common in Upper Egypt, with nobody bothering to hunt them. 'In the neighbourhood of Thebes the small boat in which I sailed up the Nile was often surrounded by crocodiles on a level with the surface,' he wrote. 'They saw us pass with indifference, they neither discovered fear, nor any cruel intent on our approach.' He did, however, add a warning: 'You must avoid thrusting your arms or legs into the stream, or you will run the risk of getting them snapped off by their sharp and pointed teeth.'

J. A. St John, travelling in the 1840s, saw a crocodile just below Sohaq, between Asyut and Abydos. In the charming book she wrote about her 'Thousand miles up the Nile', Amelia B. Edwards tells us that in 1874 she had to pass the first cataract before she got a glimpse of a crocodile. Near the Nubian town of Wadi Halfa the saurians were quite common in her time, though frequently shot at by tourists. In the second cataract, a short way above Wadi Halfa, a good number

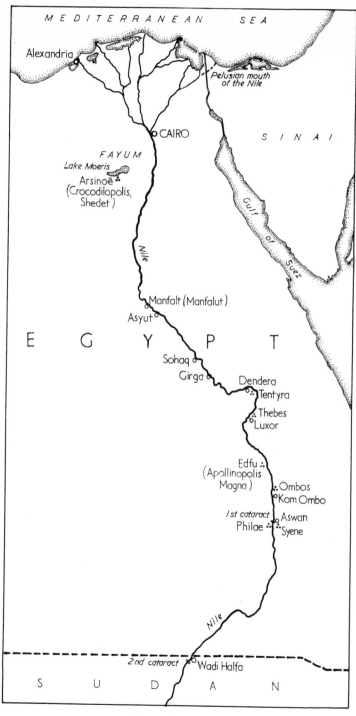

*The Nile in Egypt*

of crocodiles could still be found in the years between the two world wars, and there were occasional rumours of a lone survivor in Upper Egypt, which could sometimes be seen below Aswan. Today crocodiles must be considered as extinct in Egypt, and they have become very rare in Nubia. The changes of habitat brought about by the Aswan Dam could quite conceivably favour the Nubian crocodiles, and a few might even reappear in areas close to Aswan, where they were exterminated long ago.

The Nahr es Zerka—or Wadi Zarga—which reaches the Mediterranean south of Caesarea, was called the 'Crocodile River' by Pliny and Strabo, and this name has persisted locally to present times. Crusaders and later travellers mentioned the occurrence of crocodiles in the swamps that once extended along both sides of the river, and in 1877 a natural history collector named Schumacher obtained a 3 metre specimen, from which he took forty-eight eggs, one of which is preserved in the Senckenberg Museum of Frankfurt. The Bedouins living in the marshes occasionally reported the loss of goats and even human beings, and according to F. S. Bodenheimer five or six crocodiles were captured during the last century, some of the skins finding their way into the museums of the Palestine Exploration Fund and the Agricultural Department in Jerusalem. Solitary individuals appeared in the Kishon and Yarkon Rivers, but it is doubtful whether they ever bred there. One is said to have been shot in the Nahr es Zerka area at the end of World War I, but the swamps were drained soon afterwards, giving way to the thriving settlement of Benjamina, and nothing has since been heard of the Palestinian crocodiles.

The first explorer to enter the mountainous region of Tassili-n-Ajjer in the Central Sahara—now famous for its wonderful rock paintings—was Erwin de Bary. In 1876 he induced two Tuaregs to accompany him from the oasis of Rhat to the Wadi Iherir—or Mihero, as he called it—in which, according to native reports, he expected to find a big lake. What de Bary discovered was not one sheet of water, but a whole chain of small lakes and ponds. On the muddy fringes of these waterholes the explorer came across numerous footprints which he recognised as having come from crocodiles about 1.50 to 1.80 metres in length. The Tuaregs told him that there were bigger specimens in some lakes farther up the valley, but they refused to take him there. An enemy raiding party had been reported in the vicinity of the

Wadi Iherir, and they wanted to set off for home as quickly as possible. De Bary thus had no opportunity of securing a specimen of these desert crocodiles, and when his account was published some eminent zoologists claimed that what he had seen were the footprints of monitor lizards. It took exactly thirty years to verify and confirm de Bary's discovery. In 1906 Capitaine Niéger reached the Iherir Lakes and shot a crocodile, the skin of which he brought to the Scientific Institute of Algiers. Another specimen was killed by Lieutenant Beauval in 1924, but when Henri Lhote, one of the greatest Saharan explorers of our days, came to Iherir in 1934, the crocodiles had become extinct. The French had shot them all, the Tuaregs told Lhote, but it did not take him long to discover that the Tuareg themselves had killed off the animals whenever they had had a chance.

No crocodiles were ever found in other parts of Tassili, nor have the Tuareg legends referring to their presence among the Hoggar Mountains been confirmed. There is a waterhole called 'Ahôuter' in the Hoggar, a name often used for crocodiles by the Tuaregs, but none have been seen there within living memory.

The explorer Henri Duveyrier received native reports of crocodiles occurring in the waterholes or 'gueltas' of the Tibesti Mountains, and when the area came under French administration, it was found that the local Tedas showed extreme caution in approaching certain pools because they believed them inhabited by the scaly monsters. One guelta is called 'Dao Medi', which means 'think before you drink'. The only crocodiles reliably reported from Tibesti, however, are the ones engraved on various rock faces! In both the Hoggar and Tibesti Mountains the saurians must have existed not so very long ago, but they obviously disappeared before the arrival of the first European explorers and administrators.

Their very recent—and perhaps still continuing—occurrence in the Swamps of Menaka in the country of the Aulimiden Tuareg south of Aïr, and in the Ennedi Mountains of the southern Sahara is, on the other hand, well documented. The Machris Expedition of the Los Angeles County Museum reported crocodiles from permanent pools in the Oued Archei near Fada, the main town of Ennedi, as recently as 1961.

Georg Schweinfurth, the famous African explorer, once heard of crocodiles in the interior of Mauretania, right on the western outskirts of the Sahara. Paul Spatz, to whom he passed on this information, organised an expedition into the Mauretanian hinterland and collected a 2.32 metre crocodile from Lake Galula, a desert pool at the foot of an impressive cliff. The skin was presented to the Berlin Museum.

The existence of these small and completely isolated populations in the Sahara is not really so surprising as it might appear, for we know that a few thousand years ago this vast desert area was a region of savannas and grassy plains teeming with game and traversed by big rivers which are sure to have harboured great numbers of crocodiles. When these rivers ceased to flow owing to progressive dessication, some of the saurians migrated to the waterholes persisting in the

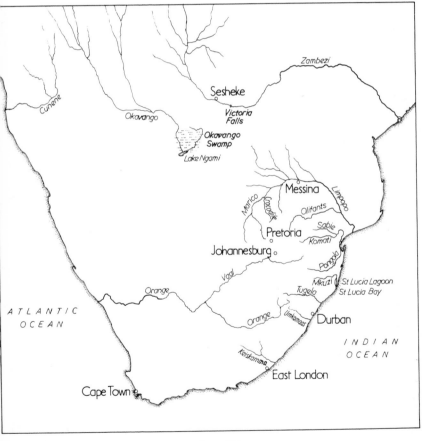

*Southern Africa*

mountain valleys. In course of time many of these relict populations must have become extinct when the shrinking pools finally dried up for good, and for the few that were able to hold out longest, the inevitable end was speeded up by human interference.

The expedition led by Andrew Smith, the zoologist, which from 1834 to 1836 explored the countries north of the Orange River, only came across crocodiles when the Limpopo system had been reached, encountering them in the Marico, the Cashan and the Oori. The latter stream subsequently came to figure on the maps as Crocodile River, but today this name is very misleading, for the crocodiles which once inhabited it have long ago been exterminated, as were those of the Cashan and the Marico. Crocodiles are, however, still found in the Limpopo, and according to Walter Rose, the South African herpetologist, they occasionally come up as far as Messina in northern Transvaal. They go much farther south in the coastal areas of south-eastern Africa and are fairly numerous in the Natal game reserves of Nduma and St Lucia. A few specimens can also be found in the Hluhluwe and Umfolozi Game Reserves. The Tugela River is often given as the southernmost point reached by the reptiles, but in 1835 crocodiles were mentioned as inhabiting the Umkomaas River, south of present-day Durban. They have even appeared in the eastern Cape, for there are records, dating back to 1903 and 1865 respectively, of crocodiles having been found in the Elliotsdale region, north-east of East London, and in the Keiskamma River, about 50 km down the coast from that town.

The present area of distribution can thus be said to extend from the Senegal River, Lake Chad, Wadai and the Sudan to the Cunene and Okavango Rivers, Ngamiland, northern and north-eastern Transvaal and Natal. On the Island of Madagascar crocodiles occur in the low lying western and southern parts from about the latitude of the Sembirano to Port Dauphin and usually not higher up than about 900 metres. There are, however, crocodiles in Lake Itasy 80 km west of Tananarive and at an elevation of 1,270 metres.

Nile crocodiles are known to enter the sea in some areas, and one was seen at about 11 km off Santa Lucia Bay in 1917. They have occasionally turned up on Zanzibar—where a specimen is preserved in the Peace Memorial Museum—and on the Comoros. Early navigators and settlers recorded them as common on the Seychelles islands of La Digue, Silhouette and Mahé, where they inhabited the brackish coastal marshes, as well as some inland swamps and streams. The saurians became extinct during the first decades of the nineteenth century. The last crocodile of La Digue is said to have been killed in 1810, and in 1819 there were none left on Mahé. Skeletal remains occasionally come to light, and R. E. Honegger, the Swiss herpetologist, was able to photograph a well preserved skull that had been dug up on Mahé.

It is, however, rather unusual for these reptiles to go very far from land. As a rule they will not cross broad stretches of open water, and when E. B. Worthington, studying the biology and ecology of East African lakes, visited Godsiba Island, about 78 km from land in the very centre of Lake Victoria, he could find no signs of crocodiles and realised that the inhabitants had never seen one. The crocodiles encountered by Worthington and his party on the uninhabited Crocodile Island in Lake Rudolf were much less shy than those along the mainland shore, their behaviour giving a definite indication that there was no mixing of the two populations.

In West Africa Nile crocodiles are found mainly in coastal lagoons, estuaries and in the rivers of the savanna areas bordering on the equatorial forest belt. In East Africa they are—or were—widely distributed, occurring in rivers, lakes, marshes and dams.

Crocodiles make their way to isolated little lakes quite unconnected with any watercourse, such as Lake Chala, at the foot of Kilimanjaro, and it is, therefore, very surprising to find them absent from Lakes Edward, George and Kivu. The Ruzizi River, which forms the outlet of Lake Kivu, descends 780 metres to Lake Tanganyika, and most of this drop is in the upper half of its course, where it makes its turbulent way over waterfalls and cataracts and through a tremendous gorge. It is understandable that crocodiles have never been able to migrate up this mountain torrent, but the Kagera River, which enters Lake Victoria and contains crocodiles in its lower reaches, has several of its sources very close to Lake Kivu, and it would seem that some individuals should have been able to cross the watershed, even though the mountains of Rwanda are fairly high and can at times be cold and misty.

Lake George is linked with Lake Edward by the Kazinga Channel, and the Semliki River flows from Lake Edward into Lake Albert. Crocodiles ascend the Semliki as far as the Semliki Falls, but have

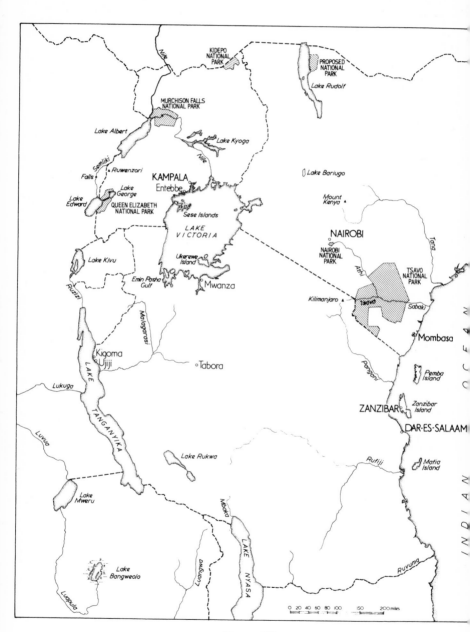

*Eastern Africa*

never managed to get past them. The falls are by no means spectacular, more like rapids, and one can think of many much more formidable obstacles that have proved no barrier to crocodiles. They are surrounded by tropical rain forest, and there are people who think that this could have kept the saurians from making a short overland detour. In its upper course the Semliki receives a number of mountain streams coming straight from the glaciers of Ruwenzori, and it has been suggested that the water above the falls might be too cold for a crocodile's comfort. Neither of the two explanations sounds very convincing.

It must also be kept in mind that the Semliki River is not the only route by which crocodiles could have reached the Lake Edward/Lake George region. The Katonga River, entering Lake Victoria, originates in the same swamp as a tributary of the Mpanga River, which flows into Lake George. A crocodile could travel all the way from Lake Victoria to Lake George without encountering any rapids or mountains, without even leaving the water. This is the kind of journey innumerable crocodiles must in course of time have performed all over Africa. We know that crocodiles inhabited a prehistoric 'Lake Edward', for fossilised bones have been found in a raised beach close to the present-day lake, together with the remains of Nile perch, a species of fish now absent from Lakes Edward and George. It is assumed that the ancient lake lost the crocodiles and Nile perch when it dried up during a prolonged period of drought. The fact that no Nile crocodiles ever came back is certainly much more of a puzzle than their recent occurrence in the Tassili Mountains.

The African Long-nosed or Slender-nosed crocodile, *Crocodylus cataphractes*, sometimes called the 'African gavial', is easily distinguishable from the Nile crocodile, for it has a high convex forehead and a long, narrow and pointed muzzle. There are four small oval scales behind the head, followed posteriorly by three pairs of keeled nuchal shields and six longitudinal rows of dorsal shields. Bony plates protect the back and the anterior parts of the belly. The upper parts are muddy yellowish to olive brown, spotted brown on the head and with transverse bands on flanks and tail. The belly is yellowish white with small black spots. The length is given as 1.80 to 2.40 metres by some authors, 1.90 to 3.80 metres by others.

The 'African gavial' inhabits the equatorial forest belt from Senegal and Gambia to Cameroon, Gaboon and northern Angola, eastwards

HEAD OF NILE CROCODILE

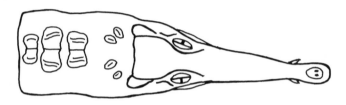

HEAD OF AFRICAN LONG-NOSED CROCODILE

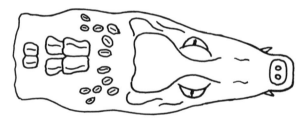

HEAD OF BROAD-FRONTED CROCODILE

through the Congo basin to the Lukuga River, which connects Lake Tanganyika with the Congo system. Some individuals occasionally venture into the lake itself. Hauptmann Heinrich Fonck of the German East African army shot one on a small island at the mouth of the Ruzizi River in 1896, and there is another old German record of one having been collected at Ujiji. In recent times at least two have been obtained near Kigoma. On a photographic safari through the northern Congo, my wife and I once came to a Mangbettu village, the huts of which were beautifully decorated with geometrical patterns and stylised representations of animals. The paintings of the chief's house were especially artistic, and I was delighted to discover, amongst fishes and snakes, a quite unmistakable Long-nosed crocodile. The species has been reported from very near the Congo-Nile watershed.

*Painting of an African Long-nosed crocodile on a Mangbettu hut in the northern Congo*

In Liberia, Ghana and Nigeria the Long-nosed crocodile is less common than the Nile crocodile. The two species overlap in the coastal lagoons and in some watercourses, but the 'African gavial' has a decided preference for the marshes and bigger rivers of the forest country some way inland. It is very shy and gets under cover when alarmed, rather than heading for deep water.

The third African crocodilian is the Broadfronted or Dwarf crocodile, *Osteolaemus tetraspis,* about 1.20 metres in length and only rarely attaining 1.50 to 1.80 metres. The muzzle is short and blunt, the eye ridges are very prominent and ossified, and the four large nuchal shields are arranged in form of a square. Between the head and the nuchal shields there are a dozen small, pointed scales. Back and belly are both protected by bony plates. Young specimens are yellowish brown, spotted black above and barred on body and tail. With advancing age they turn blackish brown, sometimes with a few lighter markings on the upper parts. The belly is glossy blackish brown in adults. The eyes are beautifully liquid brown in colour.

Two subspecies have been described. The West African Dwarf crocodile, *Osteolaemus tetraspis tetraspis*, which inhabits the forest areas of Sierra Leone, Liberia, Calabar, Cameroon and Gaboon, became known to science from a specimen obtained in the Ogowe River by Paul du Chaillu, the naturalist-explorer. The tip of its snout has the appearance of being swollen and gives it a decidedly pug-nosed profile. Osborn's Dwarf crocodile, *Osteolaemus tetraspis osborni*, from the upper Congo region, especially from the Ituri Forest, lacks this swelling.

In some places the Broad-fronted crocodile overlaps with the Nile crocodile and the Long-nosed crocodile, and it is said to be occasionally eaten by the bigger species. As a rule, however, it sticks to small streams and ponds in dense forest. On Cameroon Mountain M. Eisentraut obtained two specimens from slow flowing, muddy watercourses, not more than 3 or 4 metres broad. Du Chaillu found the dwarf crocodile to be nocturnal and solitary in its habits, and he reported it as hiding in a long burrow with two entrances, which it laboriously scraped out with its paws. The forest people of Liberia told Buettikofer, the Swiss naturalist, that the species inhabited holes dug into the banks of forest streams.

The Broad-fronted crocodile sometimes wanders quite a long way from water. Cansdale tells of one that turned up in a pit latrine a quarter of a mile from the nearest stream. In the vicinity of Buea, Cameroon, one was shot about 5 miles from any permanent water. The most remarkable story is that of an individual of the Congo subspecies, about 1.80 metres in length and showing signs of being very aged, which was caught alive in a pit near Lake George in Uganda, the easternmost point at which the Dwarf crocodile has so far been recorded.

The Marsh crocodile or Mugger, *Crocodylus palustris*, of India is fairly closely allied to the Nile crocodile. The muzzle is short, its length much less than twice its breadth at the base, almost as broad and blunt as an alligator's and without any ridges. There is a square of four shields on the nape, with four distinct scales between the large shields and the head. The longitudinal lines of dorsal shields often number only four, certainly never more than six. The colour is olive, pale, with large black spots in young individuals, darker in adults. The mugger rarely exceeds 3 to 3.60 metres in length, and one of 4.20 metres can be considered as quite exceptional. A specimen of 2.74 metres weighs about 245 lb or 111 kg. When moving about on land, the mugger often uses the 'high walk' like the Nile crocodile.

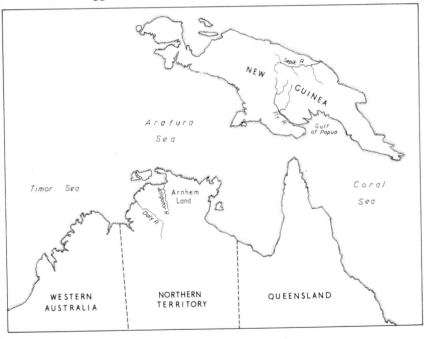

*New Guinea and Northern Australia*

The area of distribution extends from Sind to Assam and possibly Burma, south to Cape Comorin and Ceylon. The species is by no means restricted to marshlands, but feels just as much at home in rivers, jungle pools and in the artificial ponds known as 'tanks'. The Ceylonese mugger also enters coastal lagoons. As it differs from continental specimens in the arrangement of its dorsal scales it has been given subspecific rank under the name *Crocodylus palustris kimbula*.

The Siamese crocodile, *Crocodylus siamensis*, is a freshwater species ranging from the Irrawaddy, where it used to be common, through Siam to Indochina, and also occurs on the island of Java. It is somewhat less blunt-nosed than the mugger and attains a length of 3 to 3.60 metres. There is a sharply defined median keel between the eyes with a triangular protruberance in front of it.

The inland waters of New Guinea are inhabited by a species that usually goes under the name of New Guinea Freshwater crocodile, *Crocodylus novaeguineae*, and grows to a length of about 2.40 to 2.85 metres. It has a longitudinal ridge, somewhat like the Siamese crocodile, from which it can, however, be distinguished by its more pointed muzzle. In mountainous areas the species will go up to about 1,550 metres. The Philippines crocodile, *Crocodylus novaeguineae mindorensis*, with a less well defined ridge, is generally considered as a subspecies of the New Guinea Freshwater crocodile.

Johnston's crocodile or the Australian Freshwater crocodile, *Crocodylus johnstoni*, has the long narrow muzzle of a typical fish-eater. Its length varies from about 1.80 to 2.10 metres and does not exceed 2.50 metres. The inland waters of northern Australia are its habitat, and it can often be seen basking on tree trunks or rocks.

The False gavial, *Tomistoma schlegelii*, though very similar to the gavial in outward appearance, is in fact a true crocodile that has become adapted to an almost exclusive fish diet. It is the most slender-nosed member of the *Crocodylidae* and carries 20 to 21 teeth in the upper and 18 to 19 teeth in the lower jaw. While other long-snouted crocodiles have the lower jaws united at the utmost to the eighth tooth from the front, this union extends as far back as the fourteenth and fifteenth tooth in the False gavial. Webbing is rudimentary on the forefeet, but the digits of the hindfeet are fully webbed. The False gavial attains a length of about 4.50 metres and inhabits inland swamps and rivers of Malaya, Sumatra and Borneo. It is less thoroughly aquatic in its habits than the true gavial.

Textbooks allow the Estuarine or Saltwater crocodile, *Crocodylus porosus*, a length of 3.65 to 4.30 metres, exceptionally up to 6 metres. One gets the impression that a person reporting one of over 6 metres would at least be sure of a polite hearing, which is more than an

African hunter with an outsize Nile crocodile can expect: Tweedie and Harrison, for instance, accept records of 8.80 and 10.06 metre specimens from the Philippines and Bengal respectively. The Bengal giant is said to have measured 4.17 metres round its middle. It seems unlikely that monsters of such dimensions could still survive today, and even a 6 metre individual must now be considered as **a** great rarity.

*Saltwater crocodile (Crocodylus porosus)*

The Estuarine crocodile has a considerably longer muzzle than the mugger, about twice the length of its breadth at the base, and there are two prominent ridges running forward from the eyes and converging on the nose. Four large shields, arranged in a square, are flanked by one or two small ones on each side, but there are none, or only a few small and irregular scales, between them and the head. The longitudinal rows of the dorsal sheet number four to eight, with the shield less heavily ossified than in any other living crocodilian. The armour plating consists of only a small bony plate of oval shape in the centre of each shield. The colour is dark olive green or brown, often almost black above, and lemon yellow on the belly. The eye is yellow.

Mangrove swamps, deltas, estuaries and the lower brackish reaches of tidal rivers are the principal habitats of this species. Estuarine crocodiles are said to make only sporadic appearances higher up rivers, but some probably spend their whole lives in the big rivers of New Guinea, hundreds of miles from the sea, and the species has also been encountered at Boea in the Padang Highlands, about 300 km from the east coast of Sumatra. In the lowlands of the Malayan peninsula these reptiles have quite often been known to travel overland and to establish themselves in lakes and deserted mine holes. The estuarine is certainly the crocodile that takes most readily to the sea, and in certain parts of Indonesia it may even lead a completely marine existence. We might perhaps compare its habits with those of some of the teleosaurians ancestral to the thalattosuchians, and the partial reduction of the bony armour could be viewed as a first tentative step in the direction of a more pelagic existence. The largely lacustrine mode of life has given the estuarine crocodile an enormously wide area of distribution. It is, in fact, found from the Sunderbans of the Ganges Delta and from the coast of Bengal to Cochin in south-western India, Ceylon, Burma, Malaya, Siam and Indochina, through the Malay Archipelago to the Philippines, northern Australia, New Guinea and the Solomon Islands. Two individuals are known to have reached the Cocos-Keeling Islands, more than 900 km from Sumatra, one has been recorded from the Fiji Islands, and stray specimens occasionally turn up in the New Hebrides. The Estuarine crocodile has been exterminated on the south-western coast of China.

It may come as a surprise to those who associate the American continent exclusively with alligators and caimans that the New World has no less than four true crocodiles. Of these the American crocodile, *Crocodylus acutus*, is almost as much a seagoing species as the estuarine crocodile, ranging from Equador along the Pacific Coast to western Mexico, and from eastern Mexico to Guatemala, the coastal areas of Colombia and Venezuela, and north through the Caribbean to the southernmost tip of Florida. It can thus be said to inhabit practically

*America*

all countries and islands between 5° south latitude and 30° north latitude. Brackish swamps are its favourite habitat. The occurrence of the American crocodile in Florida was only made known to science in 1875, when William T. Hornaday, a budding museum collector destined to become one of America's great naturalists and conservationists, was sent out from Washington to get some alligator skins.

Having heard of a 'big old 'gator' in Arch Creek at the head of Biscayne Bay, Hornaday and his companion went in search of it. It turned out to be much more of a prize than they had anticipated. As Hornaday put it: 'In a few hours we got sight of him, out on the bank in a saw-grass wallow. He was a monster for size—a perfect whale of a saurian, grey in colour—and by all the powers, he was a genuine Crocodile!' The animal was 14 ft 2 in long, with about 4 in of the tail missing. At that time crocodiles could be found from Cape Sable to Lake Worth, but they have now withdrawn to the keys and mud-banks of the Cape Sable area. Being more susceptible to cold, the American crocodile never managed to spread as far north as the alligator. In water of 7.2°C, in which an alligator can subsist for a time without too much inconvenience, a crocodile will become so completely helpless that it drowns.

The American crocodile has a triangular, moderately pointed head, the fairly long snout having the appearance of being swollen up in front of the eyes. It grows to a length of 3.60 metres, and exceptionally to 7 metres. Individuals of less than 3.35 metres are olive brown above and light yellow on the belly, and in old age the colour turns to dull weatherbeaten grey. There are only about four rows of rather irregularly arranged dorsal shields.

Of the Orinoco crocodile, *Crocodylus intermedius*, specimens of 5.24 and 6.80 metres have been measured by Alexander von Humboldt and his companion Aimé Bonpland. The average length seems to be around 3 or 4 metres. The snout is triangular, but considerably more slender and sharp-pointed than in the American crocodile, from which species it also differs by having six instead of four rows of dorsal shields. It is found in the Orinoco and its many tributaries.

Hornaday, who collected crocodiles in many parts of the world, came across the Cuban crocodile, *Crocodylus rhombifer*, on the Isle of Pines and in the saltwater lagoons along the northern shores of Cuba. Today this species is restricted to the Zapata Swamp and must be considered as being in immediate danger of extinction. Great efforts will be necessary to ensure its survival. The Cuban crocodile attains a length of 2 to 3 metres; it has two oblique ridges in front of the eyes, which combine with the inner borders of the orbits in forming a rhomboid figure.

Some crocodile skins brought to the Paris Museum by the French traveller Morelet in 1851 formed the basis for the description of a new species, which was named *Crocodylus moreleti* after its discoverer. No further specimens of Morelet's crocodile were seen for over 70 years, and there was a growing suspicion among herpetologists that the skins in the Paris Museum might be those of Cuban crocodiles. An expedition sent out by the Chicago Natural History Museum in 1923 rediscovered Morelet's crocodile in a swamp inland from Belize, British Honduras, thus firmly establishing its status as a separate species. It attains an average length of a little over 2 metres, and the snout has that aspect of being swollen up directly in front of the eyes also present in the American crocodile. Morelet's crocodile once ranged from southern Mexico through Guatemala to British Honduras, but the species has fared almost as badly at the hands of man as the closely related Cuban crocodile, so that it now figures high on the list of endangered reptiles. It still occurs in the swamplands of Tabasco, side by side with the American crocodile.

*Alligator in Florida*

The most famous of the New World crocodilians is undoubtedly the American alligator, *Alligator mississipiensis* (Daudin, who named the species, either left out one p in error or, what seems more probable, followed a way of spelling current in France at that time; the laws of nomenclature do not permit any changes in the spelling of the name accompanying the original description). French explorers and settlers on the Mississippi and in Florida reported its existence around the middle of the sixteenth century, and stay-at-home Europeans became acquainted with it through a woodcut Theodore de Bry executed from a drawing brought home by Jacques de Moyne, an artist who had accompanied a Huguenot expedition to Florida. It shows a monster saurian, at least 12 metres in length, being attacked by a crowd of puny little Indians. The alligator later attracted the attention of such eminent pioneer naturalists as William Bartram and John James Audubon. Today its life-history is as well known as that of the Nile crocodile, if not better.

The alligator's muzzle is blunt, rounded, and so flat and smooth on top that it has been likened to the snout of a pike. In German literature the species is often referred to as 'Hechtaligator', which can be freely translated as 'pike-headed alligator'. A bony septum separates the nostrils, and there is a longitudinal ridge between the nasal openings. Two pairs of large shields cover the nape, and the dorsal shields are arranged in eight longitudinal rows. The legs are slender and somewhat weak, with well developed webs between the digits.

Alligators are rather sluggish on land, moving much more clumsily than crocodiles, and even in the water they cannot rival the latter's agility. They are also less aggressive, and Raymond L. Ditmars, a former Curator of Reptiles in the New York Zoological Park, points out that zoo keepers take many more liberties with alligators than they ever would with crocodiles. An alligator brought to bay will throw its head from side to side, snap its jaws noisily and swish its tail, but for a man with good nerves it is not too difficult to overcome and rope it. A crocodile is a much more dangerous animal to tackle. Two Cuban crocodiles which Ditmars had in his care were extremely fierce, snapping at anyone who came near their tank. 'As the food was brought, they threw the forward portion of the body high out of the water by suddenly elevating the tail,' he writes, 'the effect being a seesaw movement assisted by an upward leap. The seven-foot speci-

*The alligator's head is very reminiscent of the flat head of a pike*

mens could spring a yard from the water. The keeper was invariably careful of his hands when near the tank.' When cleaning the alligator pool the keepers often walked over the backs of some of the big reptiles—a thing they would never have attempted with any of the crocodiles.

Young alligators have light yellow bands on the tail, but these disappear after a length of about 3 metres has been reached, and the animals then appear coal black when wet and dull grey when perfectly dry. The belly is yellowish. The biggest alligator Hornaday ever came across was 'Old Mose' of the New York Zoological Park, which measured 12 ft 5 in or 3.77 metres. A stuffed specimen, 4.90 metres in length, was exhibited at the Cotton Centennial Exhibition in New Orleans, and a Louisiana alligator of 5.84 metres is generally considered as the all-time record. Average individuals vary from 2.40 to 3 metres.

The alligator's original area of distribution extended from about 35° north latitude in southern North Carolina along the Atlantic

Coast to Cape Sable, the southernmost tip of Florida, and through the Gulf States to the Rio Grande in southern Texas. In the 1927 edition of his *American Natural History* Hornaday wrote: 'To-day you can travel from Jacksonville to Miami without once seeing the black line upon the water which betokens the existence of an alligator, and an experienced Florida hunter has declared his belief that there is now not living in that state a specimen as large as "Old Mose" of the Zoological Park.' The American alligator has, in fact, completely disappeared from many of its former haunts.

It was something of a zoological sensation when Robert Swinhoe, British Vice-Consul in Amoy and a keen naturalist who brought many far-eastern animals to the notice of western science, announced in 1870 that there were alligators in China. This statement was met with a certain amount of scepticism, but the Chinese alligator was officially described by Fauvel in 1879 and named *Alligator sinensis*. After a few individuals had been sent to Europe, nothing further was heard of the species for a long time, and it was presumed to be extinct until Clifford H. Pope, in 1925, collected some specimens near the city of Wuhu, a short distance up the Yangtse from Nankin. In the course of his extensive researches into the herpetology of China he found this crocodilian to be restricted to grassy swamps in the lower Yangtse Valley.

The Chinese alligator has a snout even shorter than that of the American species. It carries two or three shields on the nape and six, rarely eight longitudinal rows of dorsal shields. There are very prominent bony ridges over the upper eyelids and thin bony plates on the belly. The length varies between 1.20 and 1.80 metres, and the digits of the forelimbs are not webbed. The colour is greenish black on the upper surface, speckled or streaked pale yellow and grey on the under parts. Nothing certain is known about the present status of the species, but it is sure to have become very rare and may even be close to extinction.

The caimans, even though very closely allied to the alligators, are quicker, more agile and crocodile-like in their movements. They also have longer and sharper teeth. Bony plates protect both back and belly, but there is no bony septum separating the nostrils, nor an elevated ridge between the nasal openings. Several species have a ridge connecting the eyesockets, that looks somewhat like the bridge of a pair of spectacles, and it is from this characteristic that the Spectacled caiman, *Caiman crocodilus* (or *Caiman sclerops*) takes its name. The spectacle frames are simulated by the swollen eyelids, which are wrinkled or may even carry blunt horn-like excrescences. This caiman attains a length of 1.60 to 2.40 metres, and its colour is olive brown above, yellowish white on the belly. Young individuals are lighter, with dark spots and transverse bands. The species, which is known as Jacaré-tinga, the light coloured caiman, in Brazil, ranges in four subspecies (*crocodilus, apopoensis, fuscus,* and *yacaré*) from the Isthmus of Tehuantepec through Guyana and the Orinoco and Amazon basins into the system of the Rio Paraguay. Hans Krieg found it as far south as the Rio Salado in the Argentinian Province of Santa Fé, at about 30 to 32° south latitude, and thinks that the caimans which have occasionally been seen in the Tigre Delta near Buenos Aires were

*Caiman at Bremerhaven Aquarium*

sick or otherwise incapacitated individuals that had been carried downriver on floating islands. Sluggish streams and bayous with muddy banks form the main habitat of the Spectacled caiman. Speaking of the Rio Paraguay in 1890, Sir John Graham Kerr, the distinguished zoologist, reports stretches where during the dry season there would be a jacaré every 5 yd or so, with here and there a group of four or five close together.

The Broad Snouted caiman or jacaré-curua, *Caiman latirostris*, has the same type of ridge between the eyes, but differs from the Spectacled caiman by having a somewhat broader muzzle. The eyelids are strongly ossified and frequently drawn out into little horns. It is a small species, attaining a length of only about 1.80 to 2.15 metres, and inhabits shallow creeks, quiet rivers and backwaters, pools and forest swamps. Its area of distribution extends from the Amazon through eastern Brazil to the Rio Paraguay system, where it is less common than the Spectacled caiman.

The Black caiman, *Melanosuchus niger*, is called the jacaré-açu, the Big caiman, by the Brazilians. With a length of 3 to 3.65, exceptionally up to 4.50 and even 6 metres, it is, in fact, the largest of all caimans. There is a transverse ridge just in front of the eyes, but the finely wrinkled eyelids are flat and not spectacle-like. The snout is as bluntly rounded as an alligator's, and the numerous nuchal shields are arranged in four to five transverse rows. Adults are black above and yellowish below, while young specimens have yellow spots and bands on a black background.

The area of distribution extends from Guyana through the Orinoco and Amazon basins and in parts of this vast region, the Black caiman must once have been extremely common. This can be seen from the account of this species given by Henry Walter Bates in that wonderful classic *The Naturalist on the River Amazon*, a book that has delighted generations of natural history enthusiasts:

> The Jacaré uassu, or Large Caiman, grows to a length of 5.50 or 6.10 metres, and attains an enormous bulk. Like the turtles, the alligator has its annual migrations, for it retreats to the interior pools and flooded forests in the wet season, and descends to the main river in the dry season. During the months of high water, therefore, scarcely a single individual is to be seen in the main river. In the middle part of the Lower Amazon, about Obydos and Villa Nova, where many of the lakes with their channels of communication with the trunk stream dry up in the fine months, the alligator buries itself

in the mud and becomes dormant, sleeping till the rainy season returns. On the Upper Amazons, where the dry season is never excessive, it has not this habit, but is lively all the year round. It is scarcely exaggerating to say that the waters of the Solimoens are as well stocked with large alligators in the dry season as a ditch in England is in Summer with tadpoles. During a journey of five days which I once made in the Upper Amazons steamer, in November, alligators were seen along the coast almost every step of the way, and the passengers amused themselves from morning till night, by firing at them with rifle and ball. They were very numerous in the still bays, where the huddled crowds jostled together, to the great rattling of their coats of mail, as the steamer passed.

On Marajo Island, at the mouth of the Amazon, there were pools in which these saurians congregated during the dry season in truly fantastic numbers. For the vaqueiros of the neighbouring cattle ranches, this was usually an opportunity to indulge in the wholesale slaughter of the densely packed reptiles. I can remember such scenes of massacre forming the 'climax' of practically every 'jungle film' with a South American background screened during the twenties and early thirties! No wonder that caimans have become very scarce on Marajo Island.

The two Smooth-fronted caimans, *Palaeosuchus palpebrosus* and *Palaeosuchus trigonatus*, are both very small, only 90 to 150 cm in length. They lack the ridge between the eyes and have the most complete bony armour to be found in any living crocodilians, the ossified shields on back and belly interlocking in a way that is very reminiscent of certain extinct species. The Smooth-fronted caimans are found in the Amazon basin and inhabit rapid and rocky streams shunned by the larger species. Their armour-plating is thought to protect them from being dashed to pieces among the rocks of the rapids.

Of all crocodilians, the strangest in appearance is certainly the gavial, or gharial, *Gavialis gangeticus*, with its almost grotesquely beak-like muzzle, set off from the head 'like the handle of a saucepan', as Hornaday put it, very slim, parallel-sided and slightly enlarged at the tip. In adults the length of the snout is about four times its breadth at the base. In juveniles it is proportionally even longer, up to five times its breadth at the base. The teeth, 27 to 29 in the upper and 25 to 26 in the lower jaw, are longer and more slender in shape than in any other crocodilian. The lower jaws are united as far back as the twenty-third or twenty-fourth tooth.

The gavial has weak legs and a very high scaly crest on the tail. It must be considered as the most aquatic of present-day crocodilians. The textbooks allow it a length of 3.60 to 4.50 metres and accept specimens of up to 6 and 6.40 metres; the largest gavial on record is said to have measured 6.55 metres, but there are unconfirmed rumours of specimens of almost 9 metres.

Hornaday writes of this species:

Gavials are the smoothest of all the large crocodiles I have been privileged to handle, i.e. all the American species save one, and three in the East Indies. They are also the brightest in colour. Lying upon the sand at a distance of two hundred yards, their bodies often seem to be uniform dull chrome yellow, but in reality the entire upper surface of the animal from snout to tail is of a uniform olive green, mottled with the former colour. Of course the older individuals lose the original brightness of their colouring with advancing age. The under surfaces are all pale yellow, the eye green frosted with black, while the pupil is a very narrow, perpendicular black line. . . . Although the skin of a large Gavial is very thick, and the entire back is covered with bony plates nearly a quarter of an inch thick, it is still as sensitive to the touch as the bottom of a man's foot. Often when watching gavials that lay apparently sound asleep upon the sand, I have seen them suddenly reach a

*Gavial in the acquarium of the Berlin Zoo*

leg backward or forward to kick off a fly that had alighted upon them. A 9 foot female which I captured was exceedingly ticklish upon the back and sides.

Gavials sometimes have a strange excrescence on the tip of the muzzle, formed by the inner edge of the premaxillary bones developing into a double knot of smooth bone that nearly surrounds the external nostrils. Of twenty-six gavials up to 12 ft in length which Hornaday collected in the Jumna River as museum specimens, not one had this knob, nor was there a trace of it on the skull given to him, and that probably came from a 13 ft individual. He did, however, notice it in a couple of gavials he estimated to be 15 to 18 ft in length but which he was unable to secure. He came to the conclusion that the strange knob was only present in males that had attained their full growth and reached an advanced age. It can be seen very well in the photograph of a big gavial taken by F. W. Champion and published in his book *With a Camera in Tiger-Land*.

The box-like hollow excrescence has been said to retain an additional supply of air, enabling the saurians to remain under water for a much longer period than usual. Apart from the fact that it looks rather small to be a really effective air container, it seems strange that old males alone should have been given this possibility of an extra-long submergence!

The gavial occurs in the Indus, the Ganges, the Brahmaputra and their tributaries, favouring broad, slow flowing river stretches with mudbanks. It has never been able to reach the Godavari, Tapti and Nerbudda systems, even though the northern tributaries of these rivers originate very close to the sources of rivers joining the Ganges. Gavials have been reported from the Mohanadi in Orissa, but Dunbar Brander could not find any in the tributaries he examined.

# 3. The Ancient Order of Crocodilia

*Turtle-fishing Indians catching a caiman* (Bates)

CROCODILES spend a considerable part of their lives in the water, and so do all their close relatives, the alligators, the caimans and the gavial. If it were possible to submit a specimen of any one of these reptiles to a biologist completely ignorant of their way of life, he would very quickly declare it to be an amphibious creature. The general reptilian characteristics would tell him that the animal was perfectly able to exist on dry land, but he would recognise it as predominantly aquatic from many special adaptations.

The limbs, for instance, are relatively weak in comparison with the bulky body, not at all the legs of an animal that does a lot of running around. The digits, five on the forefoot and four on the hindfoot, are partially, in some species almost completely, webbed. The nostrils and eyes are placed on top of the head, evidently to allow the reptile to breathe and see while remaining practically submerged. With both the eyes and the nostrils very close together, only a small area of the head has to be exposed. The nostrils can be opened and closed by means of special muscles, the inside of the nose thus being sealed off when the animal is under water.

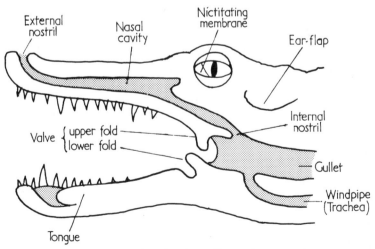

*Head of a crocodilian (based on Bellairs and Carrington)*

The adaptation of the breathing apparatus to an amphibious existence does, however, go a good deal further than this. The nostrils of other reptiles open directly into the roof of the mouth. In crocodiles this is not possible, for they have evolved a false or secondary palate, consisting of parts of the pterygoids, the maxillae and the palatines, and extending the whole length of the muzzle. The nasal cavities have been stretched out into long bone-walled tubes that enter the throat in front of the orifice of the windpipe or trachea. Anterior to the internal nares there is a broad fleshy transverse fold on the tongue, which corresponds to a similar fold or flap projecting from the roof of the mouth. The lower fold can be drawn up in front of this flap, the two forming a valve which shuts off the throat from the buccal cavity. This enables the crocodile to open its mouth under water without getting the respiratory apparatus flooded in the process, and if, at the same time, it raises the nostrils above the surface, it can also

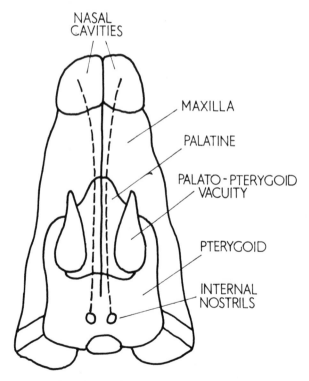

*Palate of a crocodilian (based on Swinnerton 1949)*

breathe completely unhampered. As the absence of any fleshy padding to the lips makes an absolutely watertight closure of the jaws impossible, this arrangement is, of course, of the greatest importance.

Being a lung-breathing animal, a crocodile must from time to time surface for air. In unruffled waters a short exposure of the nasal disc containing the nostrils is quite sufficient, but in high waves the head has to be lifted out of the water at a steep angle, and the reptiles, therefore, dislike rough waters. When gales whipped up high waves on Lake Tanganyika, T. Murray Smith often saw crocodiles heading shorewards with heads held high, and he noticed that they had a tendency to spend stormy days on sandbanks and mudflats.

How often does a crocodile have to come up for breathing? It is not easy to settle this point through observations in the field, but Colonel Meinertzhagen once had an opportunity of timing a crocodile in the Nzoia River of Kenya and saw it surfacing at intervals of 21, 35, and 47 minutes. There is a record of one staying under for a full hour. Hugh Cott kept crocodiles in a pond and found that the maximum submergence varied according to the size of the individual. A specimen of 1 metre once remained under water for 44 minutes. For crocodiles of 66.1 and 29 cm he recorded maximum times of 25.30 and 16 minutes respectively. Cott also experimented with very young crocodiles, which were held under water by a harness. Of four newly hatched animals, two survived a 30 minute submergence, while the two others failed to recover. A 72.2 cm crocodile still moved after 57 minutes under water and would probably have survived an hour. Clifford H. Pope mentions an alligator that was kept under water for 5 hours before it drowned. Nile crocodiles will probably not dive much deeper than 10 metres, certainly not more than 20 metres.

A crocodile's ears are placed at the same level as the eyes and nostrils, and they can be closed by means of strongly hinged scaly flaps. On emergence from the water, these flaps are slightly lifted, revealing a slit-like opening in front, which seems to give the crocodile all the hearing power it needs.

The eye has a narrow slit-like pupil, as is to be expected in an animal mainly active at night. The pupil expands in the dark and takes on a circular shape. The upper and lower eyelids are well developed, and there is also an inner eyelid or nictitating membrane. Nobody who has spent some time watching crocodiles can doubt that their eyesight is very good, even excellent. Experimenting with caimans kept in captivity, Zdenek Vogel came to the conclusion that they could distinguish several colours and see the outlines of large objects clearly at a distance of 17 to 33 ft (5 to 10 metres). They noticed movements 100 ft (33 metres) away, and were also able to distinguish objects which did not move. His animals were very young, and judging from the performance observed in adult Nile crocodiles, I am inclined to think that the eyesight increases in acuteness as they grow older and have a much more extensive hunting range.

It is more difficult to assess the reach and importance of the olfactory sense, but A. A. Dunbar Brander, author of a very informative book on Indian wildlife, had crocodiles smell and remove tiger kills at a distance of 500 ft (166 metres) from a pool. This well-developed sense of smell is of no use under water, the nostrils being hermetically closed as soon as the animal dives. Some vertebrates have an accessory olfactory organ, known as Jacobson's organ, on the roof of the mouth, but this is not present in crocodilians. There are, however, taste buds on the tongue, and some very young estuarine crocodiles of Vogel's began to hunt around for unwashed meat the very moment the blood actually touched the tongue. It is well known that Nile crocodiles are attracted by blood spilled into moving water. Vogel thought that the taste-buds only played a very small part in locating prey, his experimental animals being unable to detect non-bleeding meat at a distance. Perception could, of course, be considerably more acute later in life.

The sense of hearing is certainly good, for crocodiles are easily alarmed by noises, and they pay attention to the warning calls of Egyptian plovers, spurwinged plovers and water dikkops. Hearing also assumes some prominence at mating time, when there is a lot of vocalisation—barks, coughs, and roars being exchanged between individuals.

The swimming crocodile supplies the motive power through undulating movements of its muscular, laterally compressed tail, which is somewhat longer than the body and carries two rows of pointed scales, merging into one towards the tip. The legs are pressed against the sides, but they can come into action as rudders when the animal changes course. Crocodiles are able to shoot forward at great speed, and they have been seen to leap out of the water like big fish.

For long periods they simply float on the surface, keeping their position against the current by slow tail-undulations. When idling in quiet waters the feet may occasionally perform some paddling movements; and they are also used for scratching and for cleaning the eyes and nasal orifices.

*The 'high walk'*

Before going to the Murchison Falls in 1952 I had often watched crocodiles slither into the water when alarmed, but I was somewhat surprised when immediately after entering the Victoria Nile I saw one walking with its body completely off the ground. I soon found this to be the normal method of terrestrial locomotion, and in course of the years I have succeeded in getting a good number of photographs illustrating the 'high walk', as Hugh Cott has called it. In this gait, which is used for hauling out, walking overland and returning to the water, the limbs move crosswise, left fore and right hind, right fore and left hind, two feet on the ground and two in motion. The hindlegs, being considerably longer and stronger than the forelegs, carry most of the weight, and the sacral part of the back is at a slightly higher elevation than the shoulders. The head is usually held fairly low. The 'high walk' is, however, a rather leisurely gait at best, and when a crocodile is in a real hurry to get into the water, specially down a steep bank, it often resorts to sliding on its polished ventral shields, the legs spread out sideways and moving like oars in order to push the body along. Cott calls this the 'belly run'. He distinguishes a third mode of walking on land—the 'gallop', in which the forelegs and hindlegs move together, the hind limbs being brought forward beneath the belly during a backward thrust of the forelimbs. I have never seen this 'gallop', and Cott recorded it only four times in many months of intense observation. All crocodiles moving in this way were small specimens, between 1 and 2 metres in length, that had been surprised when asleep at some distance from the water. They bounded along like squirrels and attained a speed of 7 to 8 mph. It is certainly rather difficult to imagine a 4 to 5 metre crocodile breaking into a gallop!

Crocodilians of several species have been reported to cover long distances on land. Dunbar Brander once encountered a mugger in the middle of a ploughed field, miles from the nearest water, and watched it heading purposefully towards some jungle-clad hills. Similar observations are on record from various parts of Africa.

The horny and mostly keeled shields covering neck, back and tail are underlaid by lozenge-shaped bony plates set in the thick leathery skin. In the African Long-nosed crocodile, the Broad-fronted crocodile and the various caimans this protective armour extends to the underparts as well. The patterns of the nuchal shields and of those composing the 'dorsal sheet' vary from one species to another, the latter being arranged in regular rows. The rest of the body is covered with tough leathery scales, rounded on the flanks and oblong on the belly. The skin of the head is tightly attached to the pitted bones of the skull, without any muscular padding at all.

The skull, which encloses a brain more highly developed than any other reptile's, is large and elongate, blunt and almost parallel-sided in alligators, triangular in the Nile and saltwater crocodiles, and drawn out into a narrow pointed muzzle in the more exclusively fish-eating

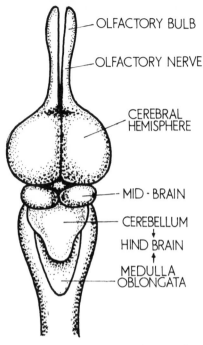

*The brain of an alligator (after Romer)*

crocodiles and in the gavial. There are two temporal openings, and the quadrate bone, movable in most reptiles, is strongly developed and firmly fixed. An old fallacy, which is revived from time to time, will have the lower jaw attached immovably to the skull, with the upper jaw hinged and movable. This can be disproved by anybody who cares to have a look at a crocodile's skull, but it is easy to see how this erroneous idea originated. A crocodile basking with its mouth open has the lower jaw on the ground, while the upper jaw is held at an oblique angle, creating the distinct impression of being mobile. This position is, however, not achieved by moving the upper jaw, but by tilting the whole head. It is the lower jaw that is hinged to the skull. The jaws are armed with a formidable array of conically pointed teeth, firmly set in alveoles. They interlock and are more suitable for grabbing, holding and tearing than for cutting or masticating. The base of a crocodile's tooth has the form of a conical hollow, into which fits the reserve tooth growing underneath it. This new tooth will eventually push out the old one, the animal thus always having a high percentage of its teeth sharp-pointed and serviceable. Even the biggest skulls preserved in museums have been found to display a full set of teeth, and it is thought that a Nile crocodile about 3.90 metres in length has already gone through 45 generations of teeth! This practical system of replacements does not seem to work so well in captivity, for even though shed teeth are frequently found in the crocodiles' basins of zoological gardens, ageing individuals tend to have big gaps in their dentition. A forty-year-old alligator in the London Zoo had only very few teeth left when it died. This may be due to some dietary deficiency, possibly to a lack of calcium.

With the jaws designed essentially for grabbing and holding prey, it is not surprising to find the muscles which have to close them very

*The skull of a Nile crocodile*

strongly developed. The muscles opening the jaws are, on the other hand, rather weak, and it has been said that a man can hold the mouth of a crocodile shut with his hands. I have never tried this and am quite prepared to accept the statement without putting it to the test!

The tongue is quite different from that of a lizard, being broad, flat and fixed to the bottom of the buccal cavity for its whole length.

The vertebral column consists of 9 cervical, 12 to 13 dorsal, 2 to 4 lumbar, 2 to 3 sacral and 34 to 42 caudal vertebrae. The individual vertebrae are convex posteriorly and concave anteriorly, the articulation thus being of a ball-and-socket type which gives the vertebral column and especially its caudal part a high degree of flexibility. The neck is strengthened by processes, hatchet-shaped and overlapping, which are attached rib-like to the cervical vertebrae. This makes it impossible for the animal to twist back on itself, but gives head and body the rigidity needed for swift, torpedo-like progress through the water and for winning a tug-of-war against animals the size of an ox, a buffalo or even a rhinoceros. With its stiffened neck a crocodile is, however, still able to turn round in a space equal to about half its length. The ribs are of a type not unlike that found in birds, which is by no means surprising in view of the close relationship between reptiles and birds. Compared with other reptiles, the ilium shows a considerable anteroposterior expansion.

Both sexes are provided with two pairs of scent glands, one being situated within the vent, the other at the throat, close to the angles of the lower jaws. These glands exude a musky secretion, the smell of which can easily be perceived in places frequented regularly by great numbers of crocodiles.

One of the most important points of anatomy in which crocodilians differ from other reptiles concerns the heart, for, in close approximation to birds and mammals, this organ has not only two auricles, but two completely separated ventricles as well. The typical reptilian heart has two auricles and an incompletely divided ventricle. On leaving the separate ventricles, the crocodiles' two aortae are connected by a minute aperture, through which a small amount of arterial blood passes from the left to the right aorta.

The gullet is large and can be used as a storage place for fish or lumps of meat for which there is as yet no room in the stomach.

The two-chambered stomach is of moderate capacity, the bigger part being well muscled like a bird's gizzard, while the other chamber appears more or less as an appendix of the main stomach, with which it is connected by a roundish hole. As crocodilians have no bladder, urine and solid wastes leave the body by way of a chamber known as the cloaka.

A great deal has been written on the subject of the stones found in crocodiles' stomachs, and various theories have from time to time been enunciated. In the course of his masterly study of the Nile crocodile Hugh Cott has paid special attention to this problem and brought together an impressive array of data. He discovered that crocodiles almost never carry stones during the first year of life, but that they all acquire them before reaching maturity. The relative weights of the stones carried by adults are always about 1 per cent of the body weight, the mean weights showing a definite increase with age. A 4.71 metre male had a load of no less than 4.766 kg in his belly. Animals living in a stony habitat acquire their quota much more quickly than inhabitants of swampy areas, but even the crocodiles of the Bangweolo Marshes eventually managed to get together their collections of stones. To find them they must travel considerable distances, and the scarcity of stones induces some of them to swallow broken glass and bits of pottery. T. R. H. Owen found pebbles in the stomachs of all the crocodiles he shot in the Sudd, the vast marshy area at the junction of the White Nile and the Bahr-el-Ghazal, where there is literally no stone to be found for hundreds of miles. The crocodiles of Santa Lucia Bay in Natal were found to carry water-worn pebbles, which they could only have picked up on a sea shore miles away. It thus becomes obvious that the stones are taken in deliberately and not just accidentally (as some people had thought).

Could it be that these pebbles assist the digestion by grinding up or triturating the food? F. Hasselquist, one of the first scientific travellers to visit Palestine, suggested this as far back as 1766, and it has ever since been the theory favoured by most authors. The young crocodiles without stones are, however, the ones feeding on prey with hard exoskeletons where trituration would appear to be most necessary. Cott also noticed that the opercula* of snails, which he took from

* Operculum: A partly chitinoid, partly calcareos plate that in some snails closes the opening of the shell.

stomachs containing stones, showed no signs of trituration. A crocodile's stomach, even though well muscled, is after all not a real gizzard. Why, Cott asked, should these reptiles need stones to improve their digestion, while so many other carnivores manage very well without them?

He finally came to the conclusion that the stomach stones have a hydrostatic function: they act as anterior counterpoise and ventral stabilising force, lowering the centre of gravity in exactly the same way as the cargo in the hold of a ship. Young stoneless crocodiles placed in deep water are unstable in their movements, both tail-heavy and top-heavy, and they cannot float level with the surface as adults so often do. The stones also serve as ballast when a crocodile lies submerged on the bottom and in dragging a big animal into the water and holding it under, their weight may be of considerable importance.

Other species than the Nile crocodile are known to swallow stones, and some notes jotted down by Robert W. C. Shelford, one-time curator of the Sarawak Museum, with regard to an estuarine crocodile, are worth quoting. 'The presence of large waterworn pebbles in the stomach was of great interest, for the place where the reptile was killed was situated in the vast delta of the Rejang River—an area made up of nothing but swamps, where one might search for a year without finding a pebble. It is evident, then, that this crocodile had travelled some hundreds of miles towards the head-waters of this, or some other river, in order to get the stones.' Shelford, who thought that the stones played an important part in the digestive economy, draws attention to the fact that water-worn pebbles have been found associated with the bones of ichthyosaurs.

Dissecting a 3.6 metre crocodile on the Orinoco, Alexander von Humboldt found eight to ten large rounded granite pebbles in its stomach. He, too, was of the opinion that crocodiles swallowed stones in the interests of digestion, but he adds the following remark: 'The Indians have come up with the absurd idea that these lazy animals weigh themselves down in order to dive more easily'.

If Cott's conclusions are correct—and to me they seem very convincing—the Indians' idea was not so absurd after all!

To feel transported back to mesozoic times at the sight of a tropical river bank covered with a dozen of these scaly monsters is by no means so fanciful as it may sound, for crocodiles do belong to a very ancient order of reptiles. The roots of their family tree have, in fact,

*Portrait of a Nile crocodile*

to be searched for in the Lower Triassic, right at the beginning of the Mesozoic, at a time when there were no birds or true mammals, a time dominated by amphibians and reptiles.

Amid the gigantic labyrinthodont amphibians surviving from the Palaeozoic and the many strange and sometimes grotesque saurians coming up in rapidly increasing numbers, there appeared some small reptiles which ran about on long hindlimbs, carrying the body in a partially upright position. The forelimbs were very short, with hands adapted for grasping. The skull structure of these pseudosuchians, as they are called by palaeontologists, was of a diapsid type, with two temporal openings separated by a bony bar. They had pointed teeth implanted in deep sockets, and from this characteristic has come the name *Thecodontia* for a whole reptilian order, of which the pseudosuchians were the earliest and most primitive representatives. The skeleton was of almost fragile lightness, with many of the bones, specially the long bones of the legs, hollow as in birds. The birds have actually evolved out of the *Thecodontia*, but that is another story! Of importance in our study of crocodilian antecedents is, however, the fact that from the *Thecodontia* arose the reptilian sub-class of *Archosauria*, which includes the *Saurischia* and *Ornithischia*—the two orders popularly known as dinosaurs—the *Pterosauria* or flying reptiles, and the *Crocodilia*.

As some of the pseudosuchians became bigger and gained in weight, they went back to a four-legged mode of locomotion and gradually acquired a protective suit of armour. The large *Thecodontia*, known as phytosaurs, and common during the Middle and Upper Triassic, had both the general outward appearance and the habits of crocodiles. Their nasal openings were, however, placed on the forehead and not at the end of the elongated snout. They were the forerunners of the crocodiles, not their real ancestors, and they became extinct towards the end of the Triassic. When the phytosaurs left the evolutionary stage, the crocodilians were there to occupy the niche they had vacated.

The earliest direct ancestor of the crocodilians so far known to us is *Protosuchus*, a reptile from the Upper Triassic of Dinosaur Canyon in Arizona, about 90 to 120 cm in length, with a small flat skull and a short snout. It had its back and belly protected by solid bony plates, and the pelvic girdle was already quite typically crocodilian. Even though it probably evolved from some primitive pseudosuchian, *Protosuchus* had gone too far to be still included in the Order *Thecodontia*. Together with *Erythrochampsa* and *Notochampsa* from the Upper Stormberg Sediments of the South African Triassic, it has been placed in the Sub-Order *Protosuchia* of the Order *Crocodilia*. These very primitive crocodiles obviously had a wide distribution, and there must have been very many species of which no remains have yet been found.

The *Protosuchia* were followed by the *Mesosuchia*, which made their appearance in the Lower Jurassic and showed a great many evolutionary advances. It can in fact be said that as early as the beginning of the Jurassic there were reptiles closely resembling the true crocodiles in most of their basic characteristics. The secondary palate, for instance, had begun to develop, and in *Teleosaurus*, one of the early mesosuchians, it was at a stage where the interior nares were situated between the incompletely united palatines. In *Goniopholis* from the Upper Jurassic and Lower Cretaceous, the union of the palatines was complete, and the interior nares had moved further back, though not quite to the position they have in living crocodilians. The articular ends of the vertebrae were flattened and slightly cupped, but not yet joined in a ball-and-socket articulation.

The mesosuchians made a very determined effort to conquer the oceans. The small short-snouted atoposaurs and the big long-snouted teleosaurs probably lived in freshwater, though some of the latter may well have been basking on the shores of Jurassic seas. *Mystriosaurus*, a direct descendant of the teleosaurs, was definitely a marine species with well webbed digits; it probably preyed on fish, squids and small saurians. About 100 skeletons of *Mystriosaurus*, belonging to the species *bollensis*, *chapmani* and *multisorbiculatus*, have been found in the Upper Lias (Lower or Black Jurassic) strata of Holzmaden in Wuerttemberg, many of them in a remarkably good state of preservation. A closely allied mesosuchian, *Pelagosaurus*, which has been found in small numbers at Holzmaden, was much more lightly built and very long-tailed; it must have been a better swimmer than *Mystriosaurus* and, as its name implies, an inhabitant of the open sea. *Mystriosaurus* was as heavily armoured as its teleosaurian ancestors, but some Middle and Upper Jurassic mesosuchians, such as *Geosaurus* and *Metriorhynchus*, lost their armour plating in adapting to a marine existence and had a skin as smooth as that of a porpoise. They went through an evolution more or less parallel to that of the ichthyosaurians, the limbs becoming flipper-like, while the long tail bore a fleshy fin-shaped lobe. Some even had a dorsal fin. Fine specimens of *Geosaurus* have come from the Oxford Clay, from Nuplingen in Wuerttemberg, and from the Lithographic Stone of Eichstätt in Bavaria. Of *Metriorhynchus* there were several species in the Middle and Upper Jurassic seas of Germany, France, England and Patagonia. The crocodilian invasion of the marine habitat was, however, doomed to failure, for the seagoing thalattosuchians, as *Geosaurus* and *Metryorhynchus* have sometimes been called, disappeared fairly soon. As newcomers they may not have been able to compete with the old-established ichthyosaurs and plesiosaurs.

Many mesosuchians never left the freshwater habitat. At the turn of the Jurassic and Cretaceous an enormous river wound its way across North America from southern Montana to New Mexico, and the marshes fringing this mesozoic Mississippi were inhabited not only by *Brontosaurus*, *Diplodocus* and *Brachiosaurus*, but also by a number of mesosuchian crocodiles that have been given the generic names *Amphicotylus*, *Diplosaurus*, *Coelosuchus* and *Goniopholis*. They must have lived very much like the crocodiles of the Bangweolo marshes or the caimans of the Amazon. During the Lower Cretaceous there were similar marshes in southern Belgium and the mining-town of Bernissart is known to all palaeontologists as the place where over twenty complete skeletons of *Iguanodon* have been unearthed. The strata formed in these ancient marshes also contained the remains of two crocodilians. One of them, *Goniopholis simum*, is a mesosuchian, the other, which has been named *Bernissartia fagesi*, shows much more highly evolved characteristics and is currently classified among the *Eusuchia*, the sub-order that also contains the present-day crocodiles, alligators, caimans and the gavial.

The Lower Cretaceous thus saw the first crocodilians differing from the mesosuchians by having a fully developed secondary palate and a ball-and-socket jointed vertebral column. Some of the earliest eusuchians were very small, *Theriosuchus*, for instance, having a length of only 60 cm, though looking a crocodile in every way. This dwarf could well have preyed upon the small mammals struggling to obtain a foothold in a reptile-dominated world. *Bernissartia* was about 80 to 100 cm long.

During the Cretaceous the eusuchians developed rapidly, displacing their direct ancestors, the mesosuchians, which faded away rapidly and became extinct. In Upper Cretaceous times the eusuchians went through a period of great diversification and produced numerous species, among them *Phobosuchus hatcheri*, a giant 13 to 15 metres in length. Without putting too much stress on our imagination, this monster can easily be seen taking its toll of young dinosaurs.

Most of the Cretaceous crocodiles were broad-snouted. A long-snouted species with completely webbed feet has become known from the Eocene, the earliest period of the Tertiary and thus of the Caenozoic. It has close affinities with the false gavial, *Tomistoma schlegelii*, which still occurs in south-eastern Asia. The very long-snouted gavialids must have split off from the other crocodiles in the Upper Cretaceous or Lower Tertiary, for a species related to *Gavialis gangeticus* has been found in the Pliocene strata of the Siwalik Hills in northern India. It was about 15 metres long. Alligators occurred in the Lower Tertiary of Europe.

The present-day crocodiles may be said to have originated in the Upper Cretaceous, and we can certainly include them among the 'living fossils'. They stuck to their freshwater habitat and never repeated the mesosuchian advance into the oceanic world. Even though some of the crocodiles living today are frequently encountered in saltwater, they show no real adaptations to a pelagic existence, and the sea cannot be regarded as their real habitat.

While the ichthyosaurs and plesiosaurs, the dinosaurs and ptero-dactyls, vanished at the end of the Cretaceous, the crocodiles entered the Tertiary in full strength and were in no way affected by the transition from the Mesozoic to the Caenozoic, which so mysteriously spelled doom to the majority of reptiles.

Politicians who flamboyantly label themselves 'progressive'— whatever that may mean—have a habit of facetiously comparing their more level-headed colleagues with the dinosaurs, gleefully predicting for them the fate that overtook these reptiles when they refused to 'move with the times'. But were the *Ornithischia* and *Sauris-chia*, the two archosaurian orders known as 'dinosaurs', really all that conservative? They produced a great number of highly diversified species and adapted themselves to many different ways of life. In their ranks could be found bipedal terrestrial predators, some of which can be regarded as the most fearsome carnivores the Earth has ever seen; huge, long-necked quadrupedal herbivores at least partially adapted to life in shallow water; bipedal terrestrial herbivores; and quadrupedal terrestrial herbivores bristling with defensive horns and protecting armour. The name dinosaur immediately conjures up something monstrous and earth-shaking, like the *Brontosaurus*, the towering *Iguanodon*, or the massive *Triceratops*, but many representatives of the *Ornithischia* and *Saurischia* remained small and highly agile. Their close cousins, the pterosaurs, even conquered the air. A space-traveller from some faraway planet reaching the Earth some time during the Jurassic or Cretaceous would certainly have considered the *Archosauria* as a generally 'progressive', very adaptable and highly successful group of animals. The only 'conservatives' were the crocodilians, which went through Jurassic and Cretaceous times with almost no outward changes. After their only attempt to spread to a new habitat—the open sea—ended in failure, they remained in rivers, lakes and marshes and restricted 'progress' to adopting a more efficient articulation of the vertebral column, an improved breathing system, a better brain and a four-chambered heart. We shall most probably never know at what point in their history this last and perhaps most important change took place, nor can we be absolutely sure that other saurians did not move in the same direction. Compared with the world-dominating dinosaurs and the flying pterosaurs, the crocodilians certainly made a very poor showing, but they survived when the much more highly diversified *Saurischia*, *Ornithischia* and *Pterosauria* disappeared. They are, in fact, the only *Archosauria* still with us. Could there possibly be a lesson in all this?

Despite the rapid rise of the mammals, the crocodilians went on thriving all through the Tertiary, occupying a much wider area of distribution than they have today. The remains of four Eocene genera have come from the Brown Coal of the Geisel Valley near Merseburg, Germany. Eocene crocodiles are also found in the London Clay and in the Bridger Beds of Wyoming. In the Miocene Vienna Basin, which began as a saltwater sea and gradually became freshwater, there were crocodiles, alligators and a 'false gavial', *Tomistoma eggenburgensis*. The climate of the area must at that time have been subtropical. Crocodiles were basking on the mudbanks of the Upper Freshwater Molasse of Switzerland, a vast Miocene lake extending between the Alps and the Jura Mountains.

The cooling of the climate which eventually led to the Ice Ages reduced their range very considerably and brought about the extinction of numerous species. Some, however, managed to survive in the regions that are the tropics and subtropics of today. Their present area of distribution extends from 34° north latitude to 33° south latitude in the eastern, and from 35° north latitude to 32° south latitude in the western hemisphere.

When an especially brainy primate, only recently evolved from an ape-like creature, began throwing spears and harpoons at them, the crocodiles gave about as good as they received and made such an impression on their opponents that they were accorded sacred status in many places. Their existence only became really endangered when the female primates became enamoured with the crocodiles' scaly skins and induced the males to go after the reptiles with such unfair equipment as high velocity rifles, spotlights and motor boats. This was more than the crocodilians, who had survived all other archosaurians by something like 80 million years, could cope with, and their numbers have been sadly reduced in the course of the last few decades. What, one wonders, would happen to the most blatantly 'progressive' political systems if they were attacked by a spatial enemy as superior in technology to their nuclear bombs as the man with a high velocity rifle is to the jaws of a crocodile?

# 4. How Crocodiles Live: Daily Life, Predation

*Egyptian plover—the 'Trochilos' of Herodotus and Pliny* (Brehm: Tierleben)

THE sun has just risen over the faraway escarpment, and its rays are lighting up the broad expanse of the African river that winds its way between banks fringed with gallery forest. From somewhere behind those parallel strips of acacias, sausage trees, figtrees and palms comes a chorus of deep coughing roars. They have a strangely ventriloquist quality, and it is difficult to say just how far away those lions are. They probably made a kill during the night and are now moving through the open savanna country in search of a place where they can settle for their digestive siesta. Soon they will be silent.

Nearer at hand a fish eagle, perched high upon a dead tree, throws back its head and utters a joyous 'Yowkow—yowkowkow'—a ringing, jubilant greeting to the awakening day. The outburst is answered from a short way downriver, and soon the two magnificent birds can be seen circling overhead. Deep sonorous grunts advertise the presence of a herd of hippopotami, and from the gallery forest come the alternating calls of a couple of shrikes. There is life everywhere, two hammerkops fishing in a pool, lily trotters running over the carpet of Nile cabbage that covers a backwater, a goliath heron flapping along one side of the river. Moving its wings in a slow measured rythm, the big bird passes a stretch of sandy, gradually shelving bank, where a couple of spurwing plovers are running about, and flies directly over what looks like a floating piece of wood. No, it does not move with the current, it must be part of a waterlogged tree grounded in shallow water. Does the early light reflected from the smooth mirror-like surface play tricks on us—or is that dark knobbly object now nearer to the bank? Yes, it is—and it has also risen somewhat higher, revealing itself as the head of a crocodile. A few minutes go by, and then the armour-plated back appears, as well as the saw-tooth crest of the tail. Suddenly the crocodile comes out of the water, walks up the bank and flops down on its belly. The time is about a quarter past seven, and the sun has already had time to disperse the clammy chill that lay over the river even after the shadows of the night had fled. Another crocodile emerges from the turgid water, and then a third. Less than an hour later over a dozen of the big reptiles have hauled out and are basking on the sand.

Even though crocodiles have a better circulatory system than other reptiles, they are not warm-blooded creatures like birds and mammals. Their body temperature is around 25°C, fluctuating within a range of about 6°C. The saurians now lying on the river bank, like tree-trunks washed up by the floods of the last rainy season, are exposing them-selves to the sun in order to restore the body calories lost during their

*A crocodile basking with its mouth open*

long night in the river. As the hours go by and the pleasant warmth of early morning turns to heat, one crocodile after the other opens its mouth, the jaws gaping widely. This is only done on sunny days and must certainly serve as a cooling mechanism, the evaporation from a large expanse of moist membranes within the buccal cavity helping to keep the body temperature at a reasonable level. Shelford records the same habit for the estuarine crocodile and adds: 'I am inclined to suppose that it is connected with the respiratory needs, for I have observed more than once that if a crocodile has its jaws tightly lashed together, and is then exposed to the full blaze of the tropical sun, it will die in an amazingly short time'.

*When it gets hot, crocodiles move into the shade*

Experiments with alligators have shown that evaporation enables them to maintain the level of their body temperature for a long time, even when near the critical maximum of 38°C. The loss of humidity can amount to as much as 20 per cent of the body weight in 24 hours, but it is quickly regained through absorption once the animal is put back into water. Of the muggers of India, Dunbar Brander tells us: 'The amount of heat they can stand is astonishing. They can be seen in May, basking at mid-day on black basalt rock which is so hot as to be unbearable for the hand. When doing this they often sleep with their mouths agape'.

At noon, when the scorching radiation beating down from the zenith becomes too much of a good thing even for basking Nile crocodiles, they either crawl into the shade of bushes and trees or return to the river. They are then often found with the body partly submerged or resting away from the bank in shallow water. Later, in the course of the afternoon, they come out again.

*In the heat of noon crocodiles are often found with the body part submerged*

As the saurians lie sprawled on the sand, absorbing warmth, spur-wing plovers and water dikkops can often be seen tripping about in the near vicinity, showing absolutely no fear of the wide open jaws. Whenever I watch such a scene, I find myself hoping that one of the plovers will walk right up to a crocodile's mouth and perform his duties as a living toothpick, in the way described by Herodotus, the Greek traveller and historian, who wrote:

> All other birds and beasts avoid him (the crocodile), but he is at peace with the trochilos, because he receives benefit from that bird. For when the crocodile gets out of the water on land, and then opens its jaws which it does most commonly towards the west, the trochilos enters its mouth and swallows the leeches. The crocodile is so well pleased with the service that it never hurts the trochilos.

Pliny quoted Herodotus, but gave it as his opinion that the trochilos was really feeding on the remnants of food sticking to the teeth. He also added the information that the bird gave the crocodile warning of approaching danger. The story of the friendship between the huge reptile and the bird trochilos—about as big as a thrush according to Pliny—had a considerable appeal and was repeated by a great many authors. Leo Africanus, the Christianised Arab whose writings were widely read in sixteenth century Europe, vouched for its truth. Paul Lucas, the French traveller, reported in 1717 that he had actually seen the trochilos enter a crocodile's mouth, and a similar account came from Geoffroy St Hilaire, one of the naturalists accompanying Napoleon Bonaparte's expedition to Egypt.

When ornithologists began to make an inventory of the birds of Egypt and the Sudan, they wondered just what species Herodotus and Pliny had been referring to under the name of trochilos. Theodore von Heuglin identified it with the Egyptian plover, *Pluvianus aegypticus*, called the 'ter-el-temsack', the 'crocodile's sentinel' by the Arabs and ranging from Egypt to the Aswa River in northern Uganda and west to Senegal and northern Cameroon. It was said to peck at crocodiles' gums—but so was the spurwing plover, *Haplopterus spinosus*, which Andrew Leith Adams and J. H. Gurney thought to be the true trochilos. Heuglin, who became a leading authority on the birds of north-eastern Africa, was never lucky enough to see either one or the other of the reputed 'crocodile birds' in action, and most of the ornithologists who followed in his footsteps did not fare any better. The old tale came to be regarded as nothing but a myth, an attitude which we find concisely expressed in a recent work on the birds of North Africa by Etchécopar and Hüe. Writing of the Egyptian plover the authors say: 'It lives readily amongst crocodiles, as we have witnessed on the Chari and even runs on their backs, but it appears to be pure legend that the bird is of service to them by picking their teeth'.

Alfred Edmund Brehm, the German naturalist who travelled in Egypt and the Sudan from 1847 to 1858 and later became famous as the author of one of the most widely read natural histories, had a different story to tell. In his *Tierleben* he gave the following account of the Egyptian plover's habits: 'Without the slightest hesitation it runs around on a crocodile as if it were just a bit of green lawn, pecks at the leeches that are bleeding the reptile, and even has the courage to take parasites adhering to the gums of its gigantic friend. I have seen this on several occasions'. This statement of Brehm's seems to have been overlooked by many authors.

Sir Harry Johnston, still somewhat sceptical after an expedition to the Congo, saw a spurwing plover pecking at the interstices of a basking crocodile's teeth on the Shire River, while Hobley reported a grey wagtail walking right into an open mouth. Hugh Cott often watched common sandpipers run up to crocodiles and snap at insects settling on their skin, and when two South African observers, Player and Tinley, told him that they had actually seen a sandpiper stand on the lower jaw and take a leech from the mucosa, he felt inclined to accept the stories referring to the Egyptian and spurwing plovers.

Colonel Richard Meinertzhagen, the last of the great pioneer ornithologists, found himself taken to task for mentioning the crocodile-plover relationship in a book on the birds of Egypt, and his critic suggested that there was probably no other authority for the old story than Herodotus himself. This brought forth a characteristic retort from the Colonel: 'I do not make statements of fact resting solely on evidence over 2000 years old'.

In his fascinating and highly informative book *Pirates and Predators*, Meinertzhagen gave the following account of what he and one of his friends had seen:

North of Khartoum I watched a large crocodile emerge from the river on to a sand bank, flop down on its belly, and open its jaws. Three Pluvianus who had been feeding nearby at once flew to it, one perching on the outer gums and pecking at the teeth. I could not say what was extracted by the birds but the whole episode looked as though the crocodile expected and invited the birds and that the birds were quite at home, inspecting the inside of the mouth of the crocodile. I also have had a letter from Peter Haig-Thomas, dated March 1950 in which he says: 'I saw Egyptian Plover enter the mouth of a crocodile several times and pick its teeth. The most interesting case was that of a crocodile 10–12 feet long, who was lying half out of the water on shingle with its mouth shut. On the approach of the plover he

*Nile crocodile and spurwing plover*

very slowly opened his mouth and the plover ran in and was certainly most of the time inside the mouth, thoroughly picking the teeth on both sides of the lower jaw.' I was on the Kafue River in north west Rhodesia in 1907 and watched crocodiles coming out to a sand bank within a few yards of me. Many came out and the procedure was in every case identical. No sooner on dry land than they would flop down, shut their eyes and open their mouths wide. The spurwinged plover (*Haplopterus armatus*) would come flying in, sometimes from a distance, and at once run up to the open jaws and pick teeth, though I never saw a bird actually enter the jaws. It has also been suggested that the spurwinged plover serve to warn crocodiles of danger, while the bird profits from the partnership by feeding on insects at the basking ground in addition to removing parasites and debris from the crocodile's mouth. Both spurwinged plovers (*armatus* and *spinosus*) and the water dikkop (*Burhinus vermicularis*) and in the Gold Coast some egret ('pure white ospreys') are recorded as picking the teeth of a crocodile.

Thus the famous story told by Herodotus has finally been fully confirmed. I have been told that a photograph showing Egyptian plovers in a crocodile's mouth was published in a German book, but my informant could not remember either the author or the title. The Egyptian plover, which, from its small size, must quite definitely be considered as the 'trochilos' of Herodotus and Pliny, does not seem to occur on the Victoria Nile—I have never seen it there—but the spurwing plover, *Haplopterus spinosus*, is common. I once got a picture of a plover very close to the head of a crocodile and still hope that one day I will be able to photograph it while toothpicking. I sometimes wonder whether the unaccountably vivid coloration of the inside of a crocodile's mouth might in some way attract the birds.

In a footnote to the chapter on crocodiles in Shelford's book *A Naturalist in Borneo*, Charles Hose states that, according to native reports, sandpipers pick something off the teeth of the Estuarine crocodile on the river banks of Sarawak. In Smythie's *Birds of Borneo*, Beccari, the Italian naturalist, is quoted as writing:

> When crocodiles lie thus with open jaws, small shore birds, especially waders of the sandpiper kind, which are always running about on the banks in search of food, enter the huge reptiles' mouth to capture any such small fry as may have sought refuge among the teeth or in the folds of the mucous membrane of the mouth or pharynx. Indeed, if I remember right, I have witnessed the thing myself; but now as I write I cannot feel quite sure that it was not one of the many stories told me by my men.

While there are no records of birds attending any of the New World crocodilians, the American crocodile has recently been found to be 'cleaned' by a fish. This is by no means an unusual phenomenon, for 'cleaner fish' of various kinds are known to operate not only on other fish, but on hippopotami as well. In Zululand freshwater turtles and two species of fish have been seen picking ticks off wallowing and bathing rhino. The American crocodile might, therefore, not be the only one to have a 'cleaner fish'.

On the Victoria Nile I once witnessed a very strange incident involving a crocodile and a marabou stork. I had asked the helmsman of the launch to steer close to the bank so that we would be able to photograph the marabou. As we approached, the stork suddenly took a few steps down the incline, straight towards a crocodile which was lying half submerged in shallow water. We had overlooked the reptile, and it was the bird that drew our attention to it. The crocodile raised its head and snapped at the marabou, but the big bird jumped out of reach with great agility, only to move forward again a moment later. As the big jaws opened a second time, the marabou's conical beak darted with lightning speed right into the gaping mouth. Before we could properly recover from our surprise, the marabou twice repeated this incredible performance, and when his beak stabbed forward for the third time, we distinctly saw it take a fish out of the crocodile's gullet. The marabou quickly swallowed its catch, and then walked away in the dignified manner so characteristic of these birds. I do not think I should ever have had the courage to tell this story, had the marabou's amazing antics not been recorded by a friend's cine camera!

A crocodile which my wife and I called 'Herodotus' lived for many years in one of the dams of Nairobi National Park. We often saw it basking on the edge of the pool, with wood ibis and spoonbills stalking around a couple of metres away and paying no attention at all to the dozing saurian. On one occasion, however, two crowned cranes came walking down to the water. When they suddenly found them-selves almost on top of 'Herodotus', the birds first stretched out their long necks to take a good look at the monster, and then began to flap their wings and to jump up and down, giving a perfect exhibition of their famous courtship display. On catching sight of the crocodile those cranes must somehow have got their 'wires crossed', for this strange dance could only be explained in terms of what behaviourists call a displacement action. 'Herodotus' never moved while this unexpected ballet performance went on in his immediate vicinity.

Basking crocodiles truly look as inert as wooden logs, and one might think that even the crack of doom would fail to awaken them, but they are really extremely wary all the time, and the slightest disturbance is apt to send them sliding into the water. They certainly pay attention to the alarm calls of plovers and water dikkops in exactly the same way as game animals react to the screech of the oxpecker or the screams of the crowned plover, though at times I have found the crocodiles more timid than the birds, disappearing even before the feathered sentinels had given the first warning. Once they realise that they have nothing to fear, the saurians will soon become less shy. As long as there was just an occasional launch coming up the river from Lake Albert, only very few crocodiles in the Victoria Nile could be approached at all closely, but daily tourist boats from Paraa Lodge have quickly convinced them of the harmlessness of these chugging contraptions.

*The sight of this crocodile induced the two crowned cranes to go through the routine of their courtship display*

One or two crocodiles are usually on view at the Hippo Pools of Nairobi National Park, and not so many years ago you had to tiptoe along the bank and take cover behind bushes if you wanted to photograph them. Today they will endure whole gaggles of chattering and pointing humans without even opening their eyes. When I recently heard a visitor from Europe refer to the 'stuffed crocodiles at Hippo Pool', I first thought this to be meant as a joke illustrating the absolute unconcern of these reptiles, but I suddenly realised that the man had quite seriously assumed them to be stuffed specimens set up on the river bank for the edification of tourists! I was all the more amused as I remembered having read that many a bullet had at one time been fired at a stuffed crocodile displayed on the bank of the Nile somewhere in Nubia.

C. A. Pooley, the Senior Game Ranger in charge of the Natal

Park Board's crocodile hatchery, gives an interesting account of how quickly even youngsters are able to adapt themselves to circumstances. When fish eagles began to take young crocodiles from some unprotected pools, the little reptiles soon became extremely wary, hiding during the daytime and only emerging after nightfall to take the food that had been put into their enclosure. They remained shy and secretive long after the pools had been wired up. The young crocodiles inhabiting the adjoining cement pools, which had always been wired up, paid absolutely no attention to the circling birds of prey, ate their food as soon as it was offered and could be seen basking in the open without displaying the least signs of alarm.

That crocodiles spend the sunny hours lazily basking and soaking up warmth does not prevent them from catching prey in broad daylight, should a favourable opportunity to do so present itself. This was well exemplified by the three saurians which stalked up to my hide on the Victoria Nile, and they would most certainly have behaved in exactly the same way if some antelope had come down to drink near their basking ground. Speaking generally, their main period of activity can, however, be said to begin with the setting of the sun. As the air cools down, they slip into the water, which will soon be the warmer medium, and in this way they conserve, at least for the time being, the heat stored up during the day. They do, of course, begin to lose warmth later in the night, and morning finds them ready to again expose their scaly bodies to the sun.

This regular changeover from the terrestrial to the aquatic habitat was well known to the authors of antiquity, Pliny, for instance, stating: 'When he has filled his belly with fishes he lies to sleep on the sands. . . . All the day time the crocodile keepeth the land, but he passeth the night in the water'.

It is interesting to find Pliny stressing the great importance of fish as a part of the crocodile's diet. Conrad Gesner, writing in the sixteenth century, called the crocodile the most treacherous, cunning and rapacious of beasts and the declared enemy of all other living things. 'The food and nourishment of these animals,' he went on, 'consists of whatever they can get: Humans, both young and old, all kinds of animals, calves, dogs and also fishes of various sorts.'

Some of the natural historians of the last century tended to overlook fish as a prey of the crocodile, listing mainly donkeys, horses, cattle, camels, antelopes, birds and, of course, the self-styled *Homo sapiens* which, according to some authors, could almost be considered as the saurians' favourite food.

Gradually, the high degree of crocodilian predation on fish began to be realised again, and as far back as 1897 Sir Harry Johnston, with a good acquaintance of crocodiles on the Congo and Shire Rivers, stated emphatically:

> The normal diet of these reptiles is fish without which, of course, they would scarcely exist, as it is only a rare incident for them to capture a mammal of any size; an incident which, given the number of crocodiles in any stream or lake, can only occur to each one at most once a year on the average.

This opinion did not remain unchallenged, and thirty years later Pitman, who himself considered the saurians as being to a great extent fish-eaters, pointed out that the question of the crocodiles' bill of fare was still a matter of much controversy. Since then, Hugh Cott and others have analysed the contents of hundreds of stomachs, and it can be said that we are now reasonably well acquainted with the feeding habits of the Nile crocodile. Fish have, in fact, been found to make up a very large part of the intake, but their importance as an item of food varies a great deal according to age and locality.

Very young crocodiles spend most of their time on land and live on insects, snapping up beetles and giant water bugs and jumping at passing dragonflies. Frogs and toads are eaten in considerable quantities until the youngsters have grown to a length of about 1.50 metres, but they do not seem to be taken any longer by individuals of over 2.50 metres.

When they have reached a length of 1 metre, crocodiles begin to turn their attention to fish, and they go on preying on them at a steadily increasing rate. The available data shows clearly that in most areas fish can be considered as the main food of individuals ranging from 2.50 to about 3.50 metres. A very substantial portion of almost any population of Nile crocodiles is thus made up of animals which are largely fish-eaters.

Good numbers of fish are caught through active pursuit in open water. As soon as a catch is made, the crocodile comes up, lifts its head above the surface, kills the fish by champing its jaws and then juggles it into position so that it can be swallowed head first. A huge and troublesome catfish may perhaps be beaten against a rock in order to quieten it down. There are, however, many ways of catching a fish, and instead of chasing after their swift and agile prey, crocodiles often lie in ambush under water, perfectly motionless, waiting patiently for an unwary fish to swim within easy reach of the jaws. The moment it has come near enough, the saurian darts forward with lightning speed and snaps it up.

Crocodiles are very clever in selecting strategic positions, where whole shoals of fish are more or less forced to swim right into their jaws. Stevenson-Hamilton gives an excellent account of two of these animated fish-traps in operation:

> During the rainy season, when the tributaries are full of water, the fish generally go some way up them to spawn, and subsequently, as they begin to run dry, the small fry come down the great rivers in thousands. At the junction of a stream known as the Mutshidaka with the Sabi there is a sand bar, beyond which the water of the latter river is rather deep. I once, during the month of May, watched two crocodiles, a large and a small one, reaping a rich harvest on this point. The shallows of the Mutshidaka, above the sand bar, were swarming with little fish of all kinds, mostly only a few inches long, which were continually being carried down into the Sabi. The crocodiles lay with their bodies in deep water and their lower jaws resting on the sand bar in about six inches of water. Their mouths were wide open, and as the shoals swam backwards and forwards, they were sucked in wholesale. Every now and then the large reptile which, of course, occupied the best place, would make a dash at its companion and drive it a little farther away, while the latter, after retiring for a time, would gradually begin to edge up again towards the special preserve.

Crocodiles of over 2 metres in length can be expected to take a certain number of mammals. As they grow larger and bulkier, they probably find it increasingly difficult to catch big fish, and mammalian prey then takes on a growing importance. In areas where there is plenty of game, the big saurians float with their periscope-like eyes above the surface, keeping a close watch upon the banks. As soon as a prospective victim is spotted near the river's edge, one of the crocodiles slowly approaches under water. Suddenly it shoots forward like a torpedo, grabs the drinking animal by the muzzle or by a leg and drags it down, holding it under until it ceases to struggle. Just as they often play the waiting game in catching fish, crocodiles will also lurk close to much-frequented drinking places, and the moment a thirsty animal happens to step too close, a sweeping blow of the formidable tail knocks away its legs and sends it tumbling into the river, where the dazed creature is utterly and helplessly at the mercy of the attacker.

This sledgehammer blow has been mentioned in practically all accounts ever written on the subject of crocodiles, yet a few years ago a professional hunter, talking to television producer Colin Willock, gave it as his opinion that a crocodile could not possibly lash out from the water level with its tail and hit an object on the bank. The mechanics of the reptile's body were against it, he asserted, and the tail was not all that flexible. Had anybody ever seen it happen, he asked.

Well, here is the answer, from the pen of Dunbar Brander, not for the Nile crocodile, but for the closely related mugger:

> On one occasion, I saw a small sounder of pigs commence to drink from a shelving sandy beach. A crocodile on the opposite bank slipped quietly into the water, and his knoblike eyes appeared close to the pig without making the slightest ripple. With equal quietness these presently disappeared, and in a few seconds the mugger rushed up the bank, and as he grounded he swung round his whole body and the tail swept two pigs off their feet into the water, neither of which appeared again.

*The flexible tail*

A crocodile certainly cannot knock an animal off a steeply rising bank while floating in the water at the foot of it. But it most definitely can and will use its tail when it is on a flat or gradually shelving shore, at about the same level as its prospective victim. It may rush out of the water as described by Dunbar Brander, but it can also attack from a position in very shallow water or from among the vegetation growing along the river bank. Stevenson-Hamilton knew several men who very narrowly escaped being thrown into the river in this way.

The flexibility of the tail is well brought out in one of the very accurate drawings illustrating Hugh Cott's delightful book *Uganda in Black and White;* it shows a female all set to defend her nest, the tail curled round, ready to deliver the famous sledgehammer blow.

Raymond Ditmars tells of the way an American crocodile, newly arrived in the Zoo, behaved immediately after having been let out of its crate:

> With a crescentic twist of the body utterly beyond the power of an alligator, the brute dashed its tail at the writer, landing him such a powerful blow that he was lifted completely from the ground. As he left terra firma, an almost involuntary inclination caused him to hurl his body away from a pair of wide gaping, tooth studded jaws, swinging perilously near. Landing with a thud on one shoulder, though otherwise unhurt, the writer threw himself over and over, rolling from the dangerous brute that was actually pursuing him on the run, body raised high from the ground. For an instant it seemed as if the crocodile would win. As the writer suddenly sprang to his feet and glanced backward, he beheld the brute throw itself flat on its belly, open the jaws widely, then remain motionless as a statue.

Mammalian prey is usually taken right at the water's edge, but this does not seem to be an invariable rule. R. de la Bere Barker heard of a crocodile racing up a steep river bank to catch a bushbuck, which it afterwards did not drag down to the water, but carried off into a thicket to devour it. A South African game warden saw a crocodile kill a donkey far from water by leaping up and grabbing its neck. Such incidents must, however, be considered as fairly unusual.

The large mammals most often taken by Nile crocodiles are antelopes, especially waterbuck, sitatunga and lechwe, which live near rivers, in marshes and on periodically flooded flats; also zebra, warthog, goats, sheep and domestic cattle. Buffaloes have been known to become their victims, and so have giraffes. Coming back from a hunting safari in Kenya—then British East Africa—Max Fleischmann, an American sportsman, sent a letter to Theodore Roosevelt describing a titanic struggle between a rhinoceros and a crocodile, which took place in the Tana River. The rhino, a full grown female, had been grabbed by a hindleg just as it was going to leave the water after drinking. Fleischmann and his companions saw it straining and heaving in a desperate effort to extricate its leg from the crocodile's jaws, and while making little headway, it did, for a time, manage to hold its own. Blood then began to appear in the water, and it looked to the observers as if other crocodiles had joined the battle, though they could not really be certain of this. After having struggled some distance down river, the rhino suddenly tried to cross over to the other bank through deep water. This was the beginning of the end, for as soon as it lost its foothold, the big animal was quickly drawn under.

Theodore Roosevelt passed the letter on to F. C. Selous, the famous hunter-naturalist, who published it in one of his books, together with three photographs taken by a member of Fleischmann's party, and with the following commentary:

> I imagine that a rhinoceros could easily be able to pull the largest of crocodiles out of the water if it was harnessed to one of these reptiles and so could get a fair pull at it from the chest and shoulders; but I think that the paralysing effect of the crocodile's hold on one of its hind legs would be sufficient for the helplessness of the animal whose struggle and ultimate defeat Mr. Fleischmann witnessed.

An attack on a rhino has also been reported from Northern Rhodesia, or Zambia as it now is. I have had a reliable account of lions' claws having been taken from a crocodile's stomach. The lion might, of course, have been dead when the crocodile got at it, but there is no reason why a drinking lion should not be grabbed and pulled into the water. A lioness in Nairobi National Park one day turned up minus her tail, and there was a strong suspicion that she had lost it in an encounter with a crocodile.

There are so many stories of dogs being taken that one might almost be tempted to speak of a 'predilection' for canines, until one recalls that whenever a dog is snapped up there is usually a human being in the vicinity to record the incident, while the grabbing of an antelope or other wild animal is, of course, only observed very occasionally. Selous once had a dog pulled under by a smallish croco-dile in a stream only about 2 yd across. The hunter immediately jumped down the bank and fired a couple of shots at the submerged reptile, hoping that the reports would make it let go. As the saurian retained its hold, Selous grabbed the dog and wrestled it away from the attacker. It had three deep flesh wounds but made a good recovery.

No predator is infallible. There are many occasions when a cheetah starts its run just a little too early or too late and finds itself unable to catch up with the gazelle or impala it had singled out; when that master of the stealthy approach, the leopard, fails to stalk up to its prey without being detected; when the strategy of a pride of lions goes awry at the last moment, and the game manages to break out of the encirclement. The lion's final rush is swift, powerful and terrifying, yet the big cat is not always successful in getting a proper grip on its prospective victim and has been known to be wounded and even killed by a thrusting horn or a flailing hoof. Mistakes are also made by the dominant predator of African waters, the crocodile.

Sir Samuel Baker tells of a 'cow that caught a crocodile'. On his way to what is now Uganda as commander of an expedition sent out by the Egyptian Government, Baker had left three cows with the chief of Gondokoro. When he came back two years later, he found that one of them had become an object of veneration, being garlanded with flowers every morning. His questioning brought forth the following story:

> She had gone to the river to drink, in a place where the bank shelved very gradually towards the water. As she was drinking, a large crocodile seized her by the nose and in the usual manner tried to drag her into its own element. Instead of this, the bank being favourable, the heavy and powerful cow commenced a game of 'tug of war', and as the crocodile maintained its hold, the cow, instead of being dragged in, succeeded in dragging the attacking party out. Nothing would induce the tenacious monster to let go, therefore by degrees, whilst struggling, both the cow and crocodile retreated many yards from the river's margin. The natives were attracted by the bellowing of the cow and seeing the position, they at once rushed to the rescue and mobbed the crocodile with their spears. They had kept the head as a trophy, and the cow was regarded as a heroine.

Verney Lovett Cameron, the first explorer to cross Africa from the Indian Ocean to the Atlantic to the north of the Zambezi, one day came upon a pile of bones which consisted of the skeletal remains of a lion, a buffalo and a crocodile. The local inhabitants told him of the tremendous drama that had run its course on the bank of the Ngombi River. A lion had attacked a buffalo, they said, and the victim fell into the river. A crocodile, attracted by the commotion, tried to catch hold of one or the other of the combatants, with the result that it was dragged about twenty yards away from the river, where all three animals finally succumbed to their injuries.

*Hippo and calf*

We all know what happened to the Elephant Child on the 'Great, grey-green, greasy Limpopo River all set about with fever trees'. Heinrich Fonck once came upon the decomposed remains of a crocodile close to a drying up pool in a river bed. The carcase was surrounded by elephant footprints, and Fonck was lucky enough to find a native hunter who had witnessed the reptile's death. As a cow elephant with a fairly small calf approached the waterhole, the 'elephant child' had run ahead and was just about to wallow in the mud, when the crocodile caught hold of it and began pulling it towards the centre of the pool. The mother immediately rushed to her offspring's rescue, drew the violently struggling reptile out of the water and bashed it against the ground before trampling on it. There is also a well authenticated record of a crocodile that was dragged ashore and trampled to death after having been misguided enough to grab an adult elephant by the trunk, and R. de la Bere Barker knew of two crocodile carcases being found in trees near the Rufiji River, thrown up among the branches by elephants they presumably had tried to attack.

In many places—on the Victoria Nile, in the Hippo Pools of Nairobi National Park, at the Mzima Springs in Tsavo National Park, to name but a few—crocodiles can be seen in the immediate vicinity of hippopotami. Among A. Radclyffe Dugmore's pioneer photographs of East African animals there are some, taken on the Tana River, which show a crocodile basking within a few yards of a herd of hippo, and one could easily come to the conclusion that there is something like 'peaceful co-existence' between the two species. A crocodile is, of course, quite unable to tackle a full grown and healthy hippo, as much at home in the water as the reptile itself, well armed with enormous tusks and fully capable of dealing with the kind of attack that proved so disastrous to the rhino Max Fleischmann saw disappear in the Tana River. A roly-poly hippo calf, on the other hand, would make an easy and succulent meal, and it is hard to believe that a crocodile would not grab such a morsel when given a chance to do so. Chances of this kind do not seem to come very often, for hippo mothers guard their offspring well and are always ready to defend them. There is some evidence that they, or other members of the herd, sometimes drive away crocodiles which show up too near the calves. Stevenson-Hamilton noticed on two occasions that the crocodiles left a certain deep pool of the Sabi River, usually a favourite haunt of theirs, when it became the temporary home of a breeding herd of hippo. The reptiles only came back after the hippopotami had left. In the Pafuri River a crocodile was attacked and mauled by a hippo, and Cott found the carcase of one at Paraa on the Victoria Nile that had been bitten in two, the body completely severed just in front of the hind legs. Only the tusks of a hippo could have inflicted that amount of damage. Young hippopotami seem to feel so safe under their mothers' efficient protection that they occasionally take considerable liberties with crocodiles. De la Bere Barker saw babies from a hippo nursery pool in the Rufiji River leap in fun on a ten foot crocodile that had come to sun itself on the bank, and they soon sent it splashing away.

There is, however, the undeniable fact that the hippo population of the Murchison Falls National Park has never shown the disastrous upward trend that led to overpopulation and overgrazing in the Queen Elizabeth National Park, where there are no crocodiles, and one cannot help wondering whether the reptiles do not, after all, have a certain controlling effect on the big herbivores. The largest crocodile examined by Cott had in its stomach parts of a half grown hippo, and five others were also found to have sampled hippo flesh. Fonck took the remains of a baby hippo, not more than a day old, out of a crocodile. It might, of course, have been stillborn, or something could have happened to the mother at the time of birth. Crocodiles will certainly attack a disabled hippo, as was once seen above the Ripon Falls, now vanished under the Owen Falls Dam—at the place where the Nile flows out of Lake Victoria. A number of crocodiles harassed a hippo that had been badly injured in a mating season battle, and forced it to leave the reed bed in which is had taken shelter. As soon as it reached the open water, the hippo was pulled under and killed amid a truly terrifying commotion. The saurians also feed on dead hippos, and altogether they must be considered as great scavengers, their place in nature's sanitation corps being hardly less important than that of the hyenas, vultures and marabou storks. Not only do they attend to any carcase that may come floating along with the current, but they also search out dead animals rotting away at not too great a distance from the river bank. Many of the crocodiles Pitman and his game scouts had to shoot on control work were removed in this way, and in the Semliki Valley four crocodiles were found feeding on a dead elephant half a mile from the water.

Domestic stock, antelopes and other game animals are by no means the only mammals taken by the reptiles. They snap up spotted-necked otters, marsh mongooses, and will devour a surprisingly large number of rodents. About forty rats were taken out of a 2.70 metre specimen, and it is known that cane rats are very commonly eaten both in Zululand and in the Luangwa Valley. In the latter region these big rodents have actually been found to make up the bulk of mammalian prey.

Considering the state of commensalism existing between crocodiles and certain plovers, as well as the amazing unconcern which wood ibis, spoonbills, tree ducks and water dikkops usually display in the presence of the basking saurians, one might well assume birds to be fairly immune from crocodilian predation. This is not the case at all, and it has been established that birds are eaten by crocodiles of all ages. The reptiles often lurk underneath the nesting colonies of cormorants and darters, and it is these species that have turned up most often in stomach examinations. Fonck frequently found the remains of marabous, herons, geese, and ducks, and he once watched an Egyptian goose being snapped up. Pelicans and fish eagles have been recorded as prey, and even small passerines, such as weaver birds, are occasionally taken.

While watching the enormous numbers of birds that came to drink at the Atbara River, crowding the low bushes along the banks, Baker suddenly noticed an approaching crocodile:

> The elastic boughs bent down beneath the weight of the innumerable flock, and the crocodile's head appeared above the surface at a distance, sank below, and quietly reappeared (the eyes and crown alone above the water) within ten yards of the unsuspecting birds, all of which were busily engaged in their twittering excitement, quarrelling for places and occasionally dipping their beaks in the water when the bending twigs permitted them to drink. In a few moments after the disappearance of the eyes, a tremendous splash was accompanied by a pair of open jaws which swept the occupants of the lower branches into the greedy throat. This artful attack was frequently repeated and generally with success.

Owen saw a medium sized crocodile scare a big flock of weavers out of an ambatch bush overhanging the water and then propel itself with open mouth through the cloud of birds, snapping its jaws shut on a number of victims. He also reports a 6 ft specimen rushing at some cattle egrets and making an insuccessful attempt to hit some of them with its tail.

The list of reptilian victims includes water snakes, pythons, monitor lizards and—crocodiles. The big saurians have, in fact, very pronounced cannibalistic tendencies and are, as we shall see, among the worst enemies of their own young. E. V. Hippel, a professional crocodile hunter who went to the trouble of examining the stomachs of no less than 587 Uganda specimens, found crocodile remains in 37 of them and felt quite satisfied that they could not have come from animals killed by him and his assistants. A battle royal between a crocodile and a python, which ended with the former as the winner, was once witnessed on Lake Victoria. Very old and decrepit individuals may, according to Cott, be only just active enough to catch turtles.

In certain areas fair numbers of freshwater crabs are taken, and the same applies to snails, which have been found to be eaten by individuals of all age groups. Large water snails of the Genus *Lannistes* form the main food of the crocodiles inhabiting the Bangweolo Marshes. The largest Bangweolo crocodile examined by Cott, a specimen 3.68 metres in length, had in its stomach no food except for ninety of these snails.

*The crocodile's grin*

We have already had a good look at a crocodile's teeth, finding them well suited for grabbing prey and holding on to it, but not for cutting and masticating. Small animals—fish, birds, cane rats, otters— are easily bolted all in one piece, but what happens to a large beast, to an antelope or a cow that has been successfully pulled under water and drowned? For a long time it was generally assumed that crocodiles were only able to deal with such prey by storing it away in a suitable hiding place until the carcase became soft enough for easy demolition.

Pitman was not so sure about this being invariably the case. 'There are numerous accounts—the authenticity of many of which seems open to no doubts—of crocodiles burying animal remains until sufficiently tasty for their liking,' he wrote, 'or concealing them in subterranean caverns beneath river banks or in holes amongst tree roots overhanging water, but I personally, during twenty years experience with these brutes, have never come across such a case'. He did, on the other hand, see a crocodile pull the carcase of an antelope to pieces, holding it down with a foot while tugging and worrying it with its powerful jaws.

It is now well known that a crocodile dismembering large prey does not only pull in the ordinary way, but grabs a limb or a lump of flesh and then rotates round and round like a revolving shaft until the part held in the unbreakable grip of its interlocking teeth is twisted right off the carcase. The saurians are thus perfectly capable of tearing a freshly killed animal apart and there is no need for them to store it in a larder in order to let it become really manageable. Yet it cannot be denied that they sometimes do take their prey into a hiding place. We have, for instance, Stevenson-Hamilton's very definite statement: 'I have often found antelopes drowned under the river bank, apparently quite uninjured, until examination brought to light the tell tale punctures about the nose'.

Having heard that our old friend 'Herodotus' in Nairobi National Park had dragged a hartebeest into its pool, my wife and I went to have a look. A couple of days had gone by since the kill had been made, but there was the dead hartebeest, one flank above the surface and, as far as we could see, still in one piece. We drove as near as we could, and I was just getting out of the car to have a better look at the carcase, when there was a commotion in a reedbed about 4 or 5 metres from the hartebeest, and out came 'Herodotus', throwing up a big bow wave and positioning himself close to the kill. The scaly back gradually sank out of sight, but the eyes remained exposed, watching us incessantly for the whole time we were there. We eventually left without having been able to ascertain whether 'Herodotus' had been busy on any part of the carcase invisible to us. Visiting the dam a few days later, we found most of the hartebeest gone, though the ribs were still sticking out of the water.

As she had obviously mounted guard over the kill for several days, it seemed reasonable to assume that 'Herodotus' had been feeding on the carcase at intervals. The stomach capacity of a crocodile is by no means unlimited, and an animal the size of a hartebeest or a waterbuck simply cannot be devoured in one sitting.

When lions have brought down a wildebeest or a zebra, they often drag it into a patch of bush, and they may stay with the carcase for up to 48 hours, tearing off some meat whenever they feel like it. A leopard usually takes its kill up a tree and hangs it into a fork in order to safeguard it from lions, hyenas and wild dogs. I have known one to feed on a reedbuck off and on for three days. The dam in which 'Herodotus' had taken up residence being quite shallow and with gently sloping banks all round, he could not possibly have moved the dead hartebeest out of sight, but I feel certain that crocodiles, too, have a tendency to pull their kills into a secluded spot. Pushed into some cavity under the river bank, the carcase can be more easily guarded from other crocodiles, and there is less risk of it being carried away by the current. Should the saurian happen to be very hungry, it may well tear off some parts of the carcase at once, but perhaps it will come up to the river bank first and continue its basking session, preferring to feed later, possibly at night. Predators do not always eat their prey the moment it has been killed. I have seen a leopard asleep in a tree, with two dead storks, still untouched, hanging nearby. Another leopard hid a Thomson's gazelle under a bush and went away, coming back to eat it later in the day.

Where crocodiles are as numerous as below the Murchison Falls a carcase must, of course, attract so many of them that the animal that made the kill will be quite unable to keep them off for any length of time. In such a place crocodile kills are sure to disappear much more quickly than elsewhere. A kill would also be more difficult to find in the Victoria Nile than in dry country rivers such as the Sabi and the Pafuri.

A crocodile frequently takes a prey to some hidden spot, not to let it become soft as was formerly assumed, but for the same reason a leopard hangs its kill into a tree—to keep it safe and handy for as long as there is still some meat to be got from it.

There has long been a tendency to overestimate the voracity of these reptiles grossly. Stevenson-Hamilton was amazed to find the stomachs of many, perhaps of most of the crocodiles which he shot, quite empty, except for a few handfuls of pebbles, and he suspected them of being able to go without food for a long time. Pitman found himself similarly puzzled when he wrote:

> Eye witnesses at the Murchison Falls on the Victoria Nile have computed that as much as a ton of fish is daily consumed by the masses of crocodiles which infest the pools below the Falls. The observers, from whom this information was derived, had ample opportunity daily to study them at close quarters. At the same time it must be said that stomach examinations—a most unsavoury task—furnished but little evidence to prove that the crocodile is very destructive to fish life.

The stomachs Pitman opened were either empty or contained only the scanty remains of molluscs, crustaceans and fish. On one occasion only did he find a full meal inside a crocodile and that was in India, where an exceptionally large mugger had devoured a wild pig after having torn it in six pieces. The suggestion that the reptiles did not destroy such enormous quantities of fish as had been assumed went unheeded, and Pitman himself had to organise the killing of great numbers of crocodiles by order of the fisheries experts. His observations, however, found full confirmation when the results of Hugh Cott's investigations were published. Of the 591 stomachs of all age groups which he examined, only 56 were replete and 83 contained no food at all.

There had been suggestions that stomachs were frequently found empty because the animals had a specially rapid digestion, but Cott could not agree with this, not finding the digestive powers of crocodiles in any way remarkable. In fact, a captive specimen, after having killed and eaten a smaller one, had the partly digested remains of its victim in the stomach a full week later. The high percentage of empty or half-empty stomachs, therefore, had to be indicative of infrequent feeding, and it turned out that the conclusions drawn from the field studies agreed well with observations made in captivity. Two 2.30 metre crocodiles at the London Zoo, which probably weighed about 45 kg each, had an average daily intake of only 365 and 280 grams respectively, and it would have taken them about 124 and 160 days to get through their own weight in food. Cott calculated that adult crocodiles do not consume more than 50 full meals a year. They are so lazy and expend such a small amount of energy that there simply is no need for an enormous amount of food. Young animals are somewhat more active feeders.

As far as destructiveness to fish is concerned, Cott has this to say:

> Bearing in mind the fact that crocodiles feed mainly upon fish only during part of their life-cycle and that eventually many other foods are also taken, we are left with the surprising conclusion that the overall daily fish consumption of an individual crocodile is less in bulk than that of a white-breasted cormorant (which consumes at least one kilogram of fish per day).

One of the most important results to emerge from the work of Cott and his associates was a scientific assessment of the part Nile crocodiles play in the highly involved ecosystems of African waters. Not only do they eat less fish than had been assumed, but what they eat are mainly fish of little importance for human consumption, or predatory fish which, in their turn, prey on valuable food fish.

The most highly esteemed food fishes of Africa belong to a group of species classified within the Genera *Tilapia, Serranochromis, Sargochromis* and a few others, but usually referred to under the collective name of 'tilapias'. In the region of the Great Lakes, around Lake Mweru and in many other places, the tilapias must be considered as one of the main sources of protein available to local populations. These fish have, of course, been caught for ages past, but modern enterprises of considerable importance and value have now grown out of the ancient and primitive fisheries, and what is not consumed on the spot finds a ready sale as deep frozen fish in the big towns. Tourists visiting East Africa will become acquainted with the 'Lake Fish' featured prominently on the menus of most hotels.

Tilapias are preyed upon very heavily by a whole assortment of other fish, specially by lung fish (*Protopterus*), *Barbus* and by catfish of the Genus *Clarias*.

In Mweru wa Ntipa, crocodiles in the fish-eating stage feed almost entirely on *Clarias*, hardly touching any other fish at all. Of 119 identifiable fishes taken out of crocodiles in the Kafue and Zambezi Rivers, 61 were catfish of the Genera *Clarias* and *Synodontes*. In Lake Albert, the Semliki River and in the Victoria Nile, below the Murchison Falls, the fish most frequently eaten are the catfish *Synodontes*, the bony, not very desirable *Alestes*, and a catfish known as 'bubu' (*Auchenoglanis*), which the locals believe to be poisonous. Above the Murchison Falls, lung fish and barbus form the main prey of crocodiles. In Lakes

Kioga, Kwania and Victoria, lung fish and barbus make up two-thirds of the fish recorded from crocodiles' stomachs, the remaining third consisting of *Tilapia, Clarias, Bagrus, Mormyrus,* and *Haplochromis*. *Bagrus*, called 'bayed' in Egypt and 'semutundu' in Uganda, is a catfish which has been described as 'quite good'. *Mormyrus* is closely related to the weird elephant-snout fish, of which Hugh Copley, a former Kenya fish warden, gave the following report: 'The writer has tried various specimens, and thought he was being poisoned. The flesh was soft, pappy, of indescribable taste'.

The Bangweolo Marshes seem to be about the only place where tilapias top the list, with seven out of twenty-one identifiable fish specimens. The Bangweolo crocodiles are, however, also exceptional in that they feed much more on snails than on fish.

Crocodiles catch a certain number of fish-eaters such as otters, cormorants and darters, while the invertebrates taken by very young individuals include a large proportion of big water beetles, giant water bugs, dragonfly nymphs and freshwater crabs, all of which feed upon small fish fry.

What happens when crocodiles are exterminated or at least so greatly reduced in number that they cease to be a factor of ecological importance? In Congolese rivers, barbus, which prey on tilapias, multiplied enormously after the virtual disappearance of crocodiles. In the vicinity of Mwanza on Lake Victoria, lung fish have become so numerous that they have an adverse effect on tilapia stocks. Otters, too, are making their presence felt to a much higher degree than was formerly the case. In parts of Rhodesia and Malawi where crocodiles have been eradicated, the crab *Potamonautes* has become a real pest, feeding on the nests of tilapias and damaging fish entangled in nets. By overkilling the crocodiles, man, in his great wisdom, has upset the ecosystem of African lakes and rivers and is already beginning to pay the price.

The Nile crocodiles of Madagascar feed mainly on fish and water birds. They are reported to take quite a lot of cattle, sheep and dogs, and have been known to raid chicken runs which they happen to pass in the course of their overland wanderings.

No detailed observations have yet been made on the feeding habits of the two smaller African crocodiles. The Broad-fronted crocodile is thought to prey almost entirely on fish, though Pechuel-Loesche, the

German naturalist, saw it grab birds which fell into the water after having been shot. The Long-nosed crocodile, too, is a fish-eater, but will also take frogs, crustaceans and possibly waterfowl.

Sitting up over a nilgai killed by a tiger on an island in the Waigunga River, Pitman was surprised when, instead of 'stripes', a mugger came to the carcase, the smell of which had attracted it from the water, 300 yd away. On the banks of another Indian river he once came across the corpse of a three-parts grown leopard, with the typical marks of a mugger's teeth. The cat had obviously been seized while drinking, but put up such a fight that the reptile had relinquished its hold.

Dunbar Brander tells us that he took the remains of leopards, wild dogs, hyenas, cheetal, young sambar, young nilgai, fourhorned antelope, barking deer, monkeys, domestic dogs, goats, calves, pigs, ducks, storks and a large variety of other birds out of the various muggers he shot. Young deer seemed to be very frequent victims. The species has also been described as very destructive to fish.

Muggers can thus be said to have feeding habits very similar to those of the Nile crocodile, and the same seems to be true of the Estuarine or saltwater crocodile, which is reported to prey largely on fish, water birds and turtles, but will also take deer, goats, pigs, dogs and monkeys.

Referring to the saltwater crocodile of Sarawak, Shelford reports:

The common Macaque, in spite of its wiliness, frequently falls a prey to the crocodile. The monkey, as I have already stated, is fond of feeding on crabs which abound in brackish waters; in the eagerness of his pursuit he draws too near the huge reptile lying immobile on the mud and looking like some old log; nearer and nearer he draws, there is a sudden swish of the huge tail, and the monkey is knocked flying into the river, where his inferior powers of swimming avail not to save him from his foe. It has been asserted by competent observers that the crocodile, if it has seized a victim too bulky to be swallowed at once thrusts its prey deep into the mud of the river bottom and leaves it there until putrefaction has reduced the corpse to such a state that can be readily torn into pieces.

We thus find in Borneo the same story as that which has for so long been current about the Nile crocodile, and it can be assumed that the saltwater crocodile, too, drags its prey to some safe place where it can feed on it at leisure.

The Chicago Natural History Museum has a fragment from the jaw of a specimen, probably about 6 metres long, which was killed by a stick of dynamite in the Solomon Islands after a long career as a cattle killer. In the Daly River of Arnhem Land, Knut Dahl found the big saurians lurking near the drinking places of the river wallabies, in the same way as Nile crocodiles watch the spots where antelopes come to the water. When Ben Cropp, an Australian producer of documentary films, set out to photograph estuarine crocodiles, a professional hunter gave him the following advice:

> Never dip your water out of a river or lagoon for more than three or four days in one spot. The cunning crocodile will edge closer each day underwater, and is likely to strike out on about the fourth day, especially if you have a dog with you. This is how most of the natives are taken.

Johnston's crocodile can be considered a true fish-eater, though it may also take freshwater tortoises, an occasional waterbird, water rats and other small mammals.

The Gangetic gavial and the False gavial are certainly the most exclusive fish-eaters among present-day crocodilians. It has been asserted that the gavial does not despise flesh as a change from fish, and portions of animals as big as a donkey are said to have been found in its stomach. The narrow beak-like muzzle and the long thin teeth are ideally suited to grab fish in sweeping sidewise movements of the head, but it is difficult to imagine a gavial seizing and pulling under water a fairly large animal. It might, of course, occasionally feed on a putrefying carcase lying in the river.

The American and Orinoco crocodiles are both quite long-snouted and can, therefore, be expected to feed largely on fish. The crocodiles at the southern tip of Florida are, in fact, known to prey upon bass, mullet and tarpon. Alexander von Humboldt found the remains of fish in a specimen he cut open on the Orinoco, but on questioning the Indians he was told that the capybara, the biggest of all rodents, was also a frequent and favourite prey of the Orinoco crocodile. Some time later Humboldt came across a sleeping saurian surrounded by a whole troop of these animals. The crocodile awoke at the approach of the canoe and went slowly into the water without in the least frightening the capybaras. When the Austrian biologist Volkmar Vareschi traced Humboldt's route up the Orinoco more than 150 years later, he obtained a photograph of an almost identical scene.

Fish form an important part of the American alligator's diet. Very young specimens feed on aquatic insects, snails and crustaceans, while larger individuals add frogs, snakes, turtles, water birds and small mammals to their bill of fare. Adults are known to have pulled dogs, sheep and goats under water. Cases of cattle killing have been reliably reported in the past, but today there probably are no alligators big enough to tackle prey of such a size. Chinese alligators eat not only fish and frogs, but large quantities of snails as well.

*Crocodiles and capybaras on the banks of the Orinoco*

Many an animal is swept into the water by a tremendous blow from the tail of a Nile crocodile, mugger or Estuarine crocodile. The black caiman, however, uses its tail with great dexterity for catching fish. In the course of his exploratory journeys through British Guyana, Robert Schomburgk frequently heard loud smacking noises coming from the rivers at night, as if the water were being slapped with considerable force. He finally realised that these sounds were caused by caimans, which killed fish and at the same time projected them right into their gaping mouths. To make quite sure of this, Schomburgk tied dead birds or large fish to pieces of wood which he set adrift. It usually did not take long for a caiman to spot the bait and to come up slowly, without rippling the surface. As soon as it found itself within striking distance, the reptile bent its body into a half circle, struck at the bait with the tail, swept it forward and snapped it up. It then submerged with its prey, to reappear a few minutes later on a sandbank or at the water's edge in order to devour the catch. If the bait was not too big, a caiman sometimes lifted its head out of the water and swallowed it in the same way as described for the Nile crocodile.

Schomburgk's observations were confirmed by Goeldi, the Swiss naturalist who founded the natural history museum of Belem, then called Para. Keeping caimans in captivity, he noticed that the tail was not only used to stun or disable a fish, but also to bring it nearer to the mouth. 'The two movements—the stroke of the tail and the snapping of the jaws—followed each other with lightning speed,' Goeldi wrote, 'and seeing how well youngsters only as long as a human hand performed this trick, I could not help being awed by the thought of what an adult of 4 metres would be able to do.'

Leo Miller, an American natural history collector, once saw a caiman corner a school of fish in a small inlet, blocking the entrance with its body. It then caught in mid-air the fish that tried to escape by jumping over the obstruction.

Young caimans kept by Zdenek Vogel, showed such a predilection for mice that they even crawled out of the water and caught the small mammals on land with a snap of the jaws. They then took the rodents back to the basin in order to drown and devour them. An adult white mouse would last a 16 in caiman from two to four days. Caimans of that length also took weevil grubs, crickets and pieces of veal. In addition to mice and meat they were later given fish, frogs, lizards, snakes, crabs and large insects, specially grasshoppers.

From observations made in their native habitat it appears that fish and water birds make up a considerable part of the food consumed by the large caimans. They also take capybaras, pakas, dogs, pigs, sheep and, of course, smaller caimans. Big specimens of the black caiman are quite capable of killing cattle, and the ranchers of Marajo Island are said to have suffered considerable losses through the depredations of these reptiles. The Spectacled caimans of the Rio Paraguay feed largely on giant water snails, their stomachs usually containing masses of horny opercula. Fish are also taken, specially the dreaded piranhas or cannibal fish.

# 5. How Crocodiles Live: Aestivation, Mating, Reproduction, Longevity.

*De Bry's woodcut of an alligator*

In the big rivers and lakes of Africa, crocodiles find a stable habitat that supplies them with plenty of food. A wide range of prey is available at all times of the year, and apart from the mating season, nothing induces the saurians to change their habitual way of life. There are, however, many smaller streams which cease to flow during the hot weather: they either dry up completely or become at least reduced to a chain of stagnant, steadily shrinking pools. With the advent of the next rains, torrential floods will soon be roaring down the river bed. An intermittent river of this kind is the Aswa in northern Uganda, where 'pygmy crocodiles'—not to be confounded with the dwarf crocodiles of West Africa—were discovered a number of years ago.

Studying the habits of these small Nile crocodiles, Pitman found that they spent the dry season aestivating in holes dug into the river banks. Having measured great numbers of crocodiles in the course of his control work, he had come to the conclusion that in a specimen of normal growth the length of the head multiplied by seven fairly closely approximated the total length. He found the head of a 'pygmy' crocodile to be 30.5 cm long, and the animal should, therefore, have measured about 2.13 metres; but its total length was only 1.52 metres. Pitman took the small size of body and tail in comparison to the head as indicative of retarded development due to the prolonged periods of inactivity during aestivation. The Aswa crocodiles must be considered not as a subspecies or race, but as runts, stunted in growth because the vagaries of their habitat force them to spend a considerable part of every year in suspended animation.

Sir Samuel Baker, who was not not only a great explorer and mighty hunter but also a very fine field naturalist, pointed out in 1890 that crocodiles remained small, never exceeding 8 to 9 ft in length, wherever they had to go into aestivation during the dry season.

Aestivation has been observed in many parts of the bush and savanna belt that runs from Somalia and the Sudan to the Niger, as well as in the Rukwa basin of Tanzania and in the dry parts of Madagascar. The burrows in the river banks can have a depth of 9 to 12 metres, and end in a roomy chamber that sometimes has a few openings at the top, thought by some to be ventilation holes, but which might well have originated through the accidental caving in of the roof of the chamber. Up to fifteen torpid crocodiles have been found to occupy one single burrow on the Songwe River of the Rukwa area.

When the last pool in the river beds dries up, the reptiles sometimes bury themselves in the mud, digging down to a depth of about 5 ft, where a certain amount of humidity is sure to persist until the rains begin. With the village tanks and jungle ponds of India evaporating in the blistering heat, muggers and Estuarine crocodiles will also disappear in the mud, and Sir Emerson Tennent was shown the 'bed' of an aestivating saurian, which had preserved every detail of its late occupant's shape and outline. Caimans are known to aestivate in certain parts of Brazil and in the Gran Chaco.

Alexander von Humboldt was one of the first naturalists to draw attention to the phenomenon of aestivation, with which he had become well acquainted in the Llanos—the savanna country—of Venezuela. In the course of his travels he was once shown an open shed standing close to a pool and obviously flooded during the rains, where two men sleeping on a bench were woken up at night by a commotion under the mud floor, which began to heave and to break up as if an earthquake were taking place. A crocodile about 1 metre in length finally emerged from the earth and rushed out into the open before the men had had time to recover from their amazement. He wrote:

> As the animals of the north are forced into a state of inanimation through the cold, so here the crocodiles and the boas sleep motionless, deeply buried in dry mud. The dry season, erronously called the summer of the tropics, must really be likened to the winter of the temperate zone, and it is a fact of great physiological interest that the Alligators of North America are in hibernation at the same time as the crocodiles of the Llanos aestivate.

American alligators do in fact spend the coldest time of the year in mud holes, about 2 to 5 ft (60 to 150 cm) deep, which they dig themselves, and Clifford H. Pope found the Chinese alligators hibernating in shallow burrows. It was by digging them out of these hiding places that he collected a few specimens for the American Museum of Natural History.

With regard to the northernmost population of American crocodiles, Hornaday, who was able to study these reptiles when they were considerably more numerous than they are today, made the following interesting remarks:

> The Florida crocodile digs burrows in the sandy banks of the Miami River and other streams where the ground is suitable. These lairs are used as hiding places, resting places and doubtless also as warm retreats in which to escape the cold waves from the north which about once every five years produce killing frosts as far south as Miami. The entrances to these burrows are either under water or half submerged, and they extend into the banks from ten to thirty feet. At their extremity they are widened out sufficiently to permit the owner to turn around. Usually the banks are so low that the top of the burrow is only about two feet below the surface.

*Crocodiles basking on the river bank*

A. C. Pooley has recorded some highly significant observations which show that Nile crocodiles inhabiting an area with a relatively cool subtropical climate will also go into hibernation. In March 1968, ten crocodiles of from 15 to 60 cm in one of the mud pools of the

Natal Park Board's hatchery stopped feeding as soon as the cold
weather set in and dug a cavern, which could be reached through a
tunnel 60 cm long and was spacious enough to accommodate all of
them. A week later, the sixty crocodiles of another pool, ranging from
60 to 90 cm in length, showed the same type of behaviour. They first
dug three tunnels, but by 9 May there were no less than nine burrows,
and unless the weather was warm and sunny not a single animal
showed itself. Even on a sunny day only the largest would come out
for a spot of basking.

Pooley had the burrows opened and found the longest tunnel to
measure 3.65 metres. Three were about 2.70 metres long, the others
varied between 1.20 and 1.80 metres. At the end of each tunnel five
or six crocodiles were discovered, all of them in such a lethargic
state they made no attempts to bite or to escape.

The winter of 1968 was an exceptionally cold one in South Africa.
I can vouch for this, for I was in Lesotho at the time, and I have never
shivered so miserably in all my life. Frost was recorded even in Zululand, and there was a high mortality among the young crocodiles
lodged in cement pools. Of the youngsters inhabiting mud pools,
none succumbed, and Pooley had all the surviving animals in the
cement basins removed to mud pools, where they promptly dug in,
choosing the south and south-east banks, where they were best
protected from the prevailing cold winds. No food was accepted by
any of the young crocodiles during June, July and August.

Burrowing always took place at night, the rapid cooling of air and
water probably spurring the animals into action. Torchlight scared
them away, but Pooley was nevertheless able to establish the fact that
they did not scrape out the burrows with their forefeet, as he had
expected, but used their jaws for the work, biting into the soft soil
just above water level and walking backwards into the pool with
each mouthful, shaking the head in order to get rid of the mud.
Three animals could sometimes be seen working on the same exca-
vation. While the burrows were quite obviously dug to serve as
shelters from the inclement weather, the crocodiles also used them as
bolt holes, into which they scuttled for safety whenever there was a
disturbance of any kind.

The burrows of the West African dwarf crocodile, which Du
Chaillu and Buettikofer mentioned, must serve purely as hiding

places, for within the equatorial forest belt there can be no possible need for this species to aestivate.

You simply cannot be dogmatic about what animals will or will not do, and instead of going into aestivation, some muggers leave their shrinking pools and wander far overland in search of more permanent water. Nile crocodiles have been known to do the same, but when the rains set in they again make their way up the tributaries, which were waterless a short time before, and even spread out over the flooded plains, perhaps settling down in distant pools where, during the next dry season, they are once more faced by the alternative of aestivating or trekking across country.

As a whole, and specially when they get older, Nile crocodiles do, however, tend to be sedentary, the same well-known individuals being seen in certain places for a great number of years. They may also be territorial, at least to a certain degree, for contests over the occupation of basking grounds or specially good feeding places have been observed on many occasions, and Pitman goes so far as to call crocodiles notorious for fighting among themselves. There must be many battles during the mating season, for male Estuarine crocodiles and alligators have quite definitely been seen fighting over females, and the same is sure to happen among Nile crocodiles.

Considering how sluggish and inoffensive they usually are, alligators seem to be quite astonishingly lively at mating time. William Bartram gave a very vivid account of a battle between two males in the wilds of Florida, which he was one of the first to explore:

> Behold him rushing forth from the flags and reeds. His enormous body swells. His plaited tail brandishes high, flouts upon the lake. The waters like a cataract descend from his opening jaws. Clouds of smoke issue from his dilated nostrils. The earth trembles with his thunder. When immediately from the opposite side of the lagoon, emerges from the deep his rival champion. They suddenly dart on each other. The boiling surface of the lake marks their rigid course, and a terrific conflict commences. They now sink to the bottom, folded together in horrid wreath. The water becomes thick and discoloured. Again they rise, their jaws clap together, re-echoing through the surrounding forest. Again they sink, when the contest ends at the muddy bottom of the lake, and the vanquished makes a hazardous escape, hiding himself in the muddy turbulent waters and sedge on a distant shore.

This description has sometimes been held up to ridicule, specially the 'clouds of smoke' coming from the saurian's nostrils—but let us remember that it was written in 1791 and about an animal very little

known and much feared at that time. Here, for comparison, is a
similar scene recorded by Raymond Ditmars, a modern herpetologist:

> A 10 to 12 foot specimen lets out a rattling bellow that shakes the night air
> of the lagoon and may be heard for a mile. When so performing, the males
> emit vapory jets of musk from the glands on the chin. This saturates the
> surrounding humid atmosphere, then travelling on an indolent air current,
> attracts company to the solitary bellower.

What Bartram called 'smoke' in the parlance of his time may
have been either watery vapour puffed out into the cooling night
air, or the jets of musky secretion mentioned by Ditmars.

The American alligator seems to be by far the noisiest crocodilian.
In fact, this was the only species of the many known to Hornaday
that he ever heard make a vocal sound of any kind. He tells us that
whenever the five alligators in the pond of the New York Zoological
Park's reptile house heard the whistle announcing closing time, they
lifted their heads out of the water at an angle of 45 degrees and bellowed,
or roared, in concert four or five times.

Caimans may not be quite as vocal as alligators, but they, too, have
been reported to roar loudly and fairly frequently. The Nile crocodile,
however, is heard much less often. Blainey Percival, with a very long
experience of the African bush, calls it a silent beast and admits that
he was never able to assign to it any of the weird noises coming from
the rivers at night. His work as a game ranger was mainly within
Kenya, where crocodiles are not as common as, for instance, in some
parts of Uganda. People who have spent a considerable time on a
river literally swarming with crocodiles, such as the Victoria Nile,
speak of the impressive roars that can be heard during the mating
season and mostly at night.

The male crocodile's roar is uttered with the head lifted and jaws
wide open. Hugh Cott characterises it as a 'growling rumble, very
deep in pitch, rattling, vibrant and sonorous, like distant thunder or
the roll of a big drum which is protracted and may persist for six or
seven seconds'. The female responds to the male's roar with a call
that is described as a growling roar rising in a crescendo by Cott,
as a series of creaks and groans by Bere.

Cott knew a native hunter at Butiaba who was able to attract
crocodiles by producing an imitation of the mating roar. This 'crocodile
call' was a vocal effort supported by some drumming. When Knut

Dahl collected natural history specimens on the Daly River of Arnhem Land, the aborigines uttered booming noises in order to make the Estuarine crocodiles reveal their presence by answering back. During the breeding season Cott often heard basking males bark or cough in deep, loud, hollow and abrupt notes.

The odoriferous secretion of the musk glands is sure to play an important part in bringing the sexes together. Opinions differ with regard to the intensity of this smell, but I have been to a breeding and hauling-out place on the Victoria Nile where it could be perceived very distinctly.

Herbert Rittlinger, the German canoeist, tells an interesting story that may possibly throw some light on the attractiveness of this musky secretion. A few years ago, he and his wife, together with two other canoeists, tried to paddle through the highly spectacular gorges of the Blue Nile. The party set out in three canoes, two single-seaters and a double-seater, and the enterprise very nearly came to grief right at the beginning, when one night a crocodile went for Mrs Rittlinger's boat as it lay tied up along the bank close to the camping site. There was a big salami in the canoe, specially smoked for the tropics, and the reptile may have tried to get at this delicacy; it did considerable damage chewing up the stern before it was discovered and chased away. The canoeists found that the boat could be repaired with the materials at their disposal, and the descent of the river was continued. All went well until the party reached a completely unin-habited stretch of the river swarming with crocodiles, and there, within quite a short time, Mrs Rittlinger's canoe was attacked twice in succession. One saurian came up from behind and had to be beaten off with a paddle, the other shot towards the canoe like a torpedo, the impact of the collision lifting the boat so high that Mrs Rittlinger was thrown forward with great violence. After this she quite under-standably had had enough of the Blue Nile, and the trip was abandonded.

Why had the crocodiles attacked only one boat out of the three? Here is Rittlinger's own opinion:

> Crocodiles exude a penetrating musk-like smell. The source is a substance secreted by four glands: two of them in the rectum and two on the throat. Normally they look like collapsed rubber balls. But when the animal is excited—in the mating season or when it is frightened or angry—they blow up like ping-pong balls and exude their frightful secretion. During the

mating season they probably squirt it in the air. Even when crocodiles creep along a river bed they leave a musky trail to attract their partners. The stench sticks persistently to anything with which they come in contact. Probably it has qualities which only a crocodile can appreciate—qualities which water can never wash off. That first crocodile—the one that got at my wife's boat during the night—was probably frightened and angered when we disturbed him, and left this uncanny scent on the rudder. The other crocodiles must have smelled it. And that is why they hurled themselves upon it with their evil grins—it could be one explanation. But we shall never be sure.

It certainly is an explanation that makes sense.

The Nile crocodile's mating habits are still very little known. People who have studied the species for many months are much less certain of what actually happens than Sonnini was in 1799 when he wrote: 'The female, which in the act of copulation is laid on her back, has much difficulty in rising again; it is even said that she can neither change her position nor turn without the assistance of the male'. He was obviously not talking from personal observation, but simply repeating a belief held for a very long time, for Gesner had told exactly the same story over 200 years earlier.

Cott once saw one of two crocodiles thrust its head and forequarters out of shallow water, the mouth wide agape, and utter a creaking or groaning sound. It was immediately approached by the other crocodile and mounted from behind. Cott does not seem to have had a very clear view of the animals, for he gives no account of the way in which they copulated, but we are probably fairly safe in assuming that the mechanics of mating are similar to what has been recorded for the American alligator: the male holds the female firmly by the nape of the neck with his forelimbs and then bends the posterior part of the body to one side and under the female, until his cloaka comes into contact with hers.

The female selects a nesting site on a sandy spit or a small island, in a dry river bed or on a flat stretch of lake shore, or, sometimes, on top of a high river bank a good 15 metres above the water. The place may be open, but it is more often somewhat scrubby, and there are sure to be trees or big bushes nearby. It will never be situated in actual forest, and the presence of a dense growth of trees can force the female to search for a reasonably good spot a few hundred metres away from the river, though nests are as a rule placed near permanent waters. With regard to soil, the female shows no definite preference—as long as it is warm and damp and has a sufficient depth, it does not much matter whether it consists of finely sorted silt, coarse sand, clay, black mould, sand loam or even gravel.

When she has made her choice, she digs a pit about half a metre deep in which to lay her eggs. This seems mostly to happen at night or in the early hours of the morning, and we know very little about the actual procedure.

*Nest and eggs of a Nile crocodile*

A Nile crocodile's eggs measure about 9×6 cm. They are equal at both ends and have a hard calcareous shell, glossy and deeply pitted. Cott recorded clutches ranging from 25 to 95, with a mean clutch size of 55 to 56. Seventy-five Zululand clutches were found to number from 18 to 91 eggs, the average being 45. The clutch size seems to increase as crocodiles grow older and bigger, for a 2.75 metre female, which has just reached maturity, never produces more than about

35 eggs. Clutches of over 80 are, however, decidedly uncommon. The female does not drop the eggs into the nest anyhow, but deposits them in tiers; and the loose soil which accidentally falls in from the rim while she is laying—or is shovelled in on purpose—covers up the various layers. Even though fairly closely packed, the eggs are thus nevertheless isolated from each other, so that there is little danger of the shells cracking through being pressed together. In the nests Pooley examined along the Pongola River and in St Lucia Bay, the eggs were almost invariably arranged in three layers. The one exception was a nest in which 91 eggs were deposited in six layers. Pooley suspected this big clutch to have come from two females, for the upper three layers contained 35 small eggs, while the bottom layers were composed of 56 eggs of normal size. It turned out that only six of the small eggs were fertile.

As soon as the last egg has been laid, the female proceeds to cover up the pit in such a way that the top layer is about 20 to 40 cm below the surface. The actual depth of the nest depends to a certain degree on the consistency of the soil, and this seems to be specially noticeable in Zululand. In the fine-grained dirty white soil bordering St Lucia Bay, which gets so hot that a person can hardly walk on it with bare feet, the top tiers of eggs were at an average depth of 40 cm. In black clay and alluvial silt on the banks of the Pongola, the uppermost eggs were found about 30 cm below the surface, while a depth of 10 cm only was recorded for nests in the finely sorted silt of an old river bed. When she has filled in the cavity, the female rams the soil tight by tamping it down with her scaly belly, at the same time moving around on top of the nest, smoothing the place and erasing all traces of her work.

Where crocodiles are very numerous, good breeding grounds may be literally crowded with nests. I have come across at least half a dozen old pits close to each other on a small island opposite Fajao, and Cott recorded no less than twenty-four in an area of 26 × 24 yd on Lake Albert. Communal breeding sites have also been seen on Lake Victoria, Lake Rudolf and Lake Nyasa.

Contrary to what has often been assumed, the female does not simply leave the eggs to their fate and to the incubating warmth of the sun, but remains in the vicinity day and night and mounts guard over the nest, either by lying practically on top of it, or watching the site from a nearby patch of shade. This, of course, is the reason why nests are always close to some trees or to a clump of bushes and never on absolutely shadeless flats. It appears that for the duration of the incubation period the female even abstains from feeding, for in all crocodiles shot while doing guard duty the stomach has been found to be completely empty. When surprised at the nest, the female utters a low threatening growl.

She possibly micturates on the nesting site in order to give the soil the required degree of dampness. An excess of humidity is, however, harmful to the eggs, and they would be destroyed if the breeding ground were flooded by the rising waters of the river or lake. To prevent such a catastrophe, eggs are usually laid after the beginning of the dry season, at a time when water levels are steadily falling. The seasonal pattern of wet and dry weather varies greatly in different parts of Africa, and so, naturally, does the breeding season of the Nile crocodile. On Lake Kioga and on the upper Victoria Nile it falls into the second fortnight of December, on Lake Albert and on the lower Victoria Nile into the last days of December and the first part of January. In Nubia and on the Bahr-el-Gebel egg-laying is said to take place in April, and in Sierra Leone during January and February. In the lower part of the Ruzizi valley R. Hoier recorded finding eggs between April and August, with the majority of young hatching during the latter months. On the Ulanga Plains of Tanzania clutches have been reported in November, while the crocodiles of the Bangweolo Marshes nest towards the end of August and at the beginning of September. Breeding is reported for the first weeks of September on Lake Mweru and on the Kafue and Luangwa Rivers, and from the beginning of November to about mid-December in eastern Transvaal. In Madagascar eggs are laid from end-August to end-September according to Voeltzkow, in October according to Decary.

On the northern shores of Lake Victoria there are two breeding seasons, one in August and early September, the other in December and January. Both coincide with a slight lowering of the water level. The crocodiles of Zululand are exceptional in breeding when the rivers are rising. Pooley even goes so far as to say that high river levels are necessary for egg-laying, which begins on 5 November and goes on to 26 December, the hatchlings leaving the nests between 27 January and 26 March. The dry season falls into the months of the southern autumn and winter, while rainfall occurs from September to March.

During December, January, February and March, high temperatures and a considerable amount of precipitation can be expected. In 1963 and in 1966–7 the rains were so heavy that there was extensive flooding of the crocodile breeding places along the Pongola River where it flows through the Ndumu Reserve, with the result that all the clutches were destroyed.

As far as crocodiles are concerned, Zululand is a marginal area where winter temperatures can drop so low that the vulnerable youngsters have to go into hibernation in order to survive. No eggs, therefore, could hatch during the dry months, and the saurians are forced to postpone breeding activities until the advent of the warm and rainy weather, irrespective of the danger high water may bring to their nests. It surely is not so much the high-water levels that are necessary for egg-laying, but rather the high temperatures that come with the rainy season.

Unseasonal floods are by no means the only danger threatening crocodiles' eggs, for they are eaten with relish by a great many animals, and regardless of the care the female takes over burying them and the close watch she keeps over the nest, a large percentage of the clutches are eventually found and destroyed by predators. The greatest and most successful robber of crocodiles' nests is the Nile monitor (*Varanus niloticus*), a lizard up to about 1.70 metres in length, dark green or olive brown in colour, with transverse rows of yellow ring-shaped markings on the body and yellow bands on the tail. It is widely distributed and quite common along most of Africa's lakes and rivers, though it is occasionally met with at some distance from water. There can be absolutely no doubt about the regulating effect monitors have on crocodile populations.

G. D. Hale Carpenter, a naturalist who spent several years on Lake Victoria studying tsetse flies, pointed out in 1920 that crocodiles were quite amazingly scarce in the Sese Archipelago, and on most neighbouring islands, while monitors could everywhere be encountered in abundance. Of all the crocodiles' nests which he discovered and visited a second time, not one escaped being raided, and even though he never caught a monitor in the act, the tracks on and around the nesting sites were quite unmistakable. On Tavu Island, which had more crocodiles than any other place Hale Carpenter explored, monitors seemed to be exceptionally rare. These observations have since found full confirmation in other parts of Africa, particularly in Zululand and Zambia. In the last-named country the majority of clutches are said to be destroyed by monitors.

A number of people have been lucky enough to photograph monitors plundering crocodiles' nests. The first to do so was I. Alden Loring, one of the naturalists attached to the Smithsonian African Expedition of 1909 and 1910, and Theodore Roosevelt, the leader of this highly important scientific enterprise, has given an interesting account of the incident:

> One morning Loring surprised a monitor which had just uncovered some crocodile's eggs on a small, sandy beach. The eggs, about 30 in number, were buried in rather shallow fashion, so that the monitor readily uncovered them. The monitor had one of the eggs transversely in its mouth, and, head erect, was marching off with it. As soon as it saw Loring, it dropped the egg and walked off into the reeds; in a few minutes it returned, took another egg and walked off into the bushes, where it broke the shell, swallowed the yolk, and at once returned to the nest for another egg. Loring took me out to see the feat repeated, replenishing the rifled nest with eggs taken from a crocodile the doctor had shot, and I was delighted to watch from our hiding place the big lizard as it cautiously approached, seized an egg, and then retired to cover with its booty.

It seems strange that so many clutches should be robbed despite the close guard kept over them, but the mother crocodile at times tends to fall into a state of torpor in which lying on the nest is practically her only defence against marauders, even though a monitor may be scraping up the soil almost at her side. The big lizards sometimes work with considerable cunning. Pitman writes:

> The antics of these prehistoric-looking creatures are most entertaining, and on more than one occasion when observing from concealment the behaviour of guardian females on the breeding grounds, I have seen one of these lizards deliberately provoke a crocodile until the latter rushes in pursuit and chases it into the water. In the meantime the monitor's mate arrives on the scene, excavates the nest with remarkable speed and starts gobbling up the eggs, in which it is soon joined by Number One, which had only taken to the water as a ruse. The lizards usually succeed in disposing of the greater portion of the eggs before the return of the rightful owner. Even when forced to withdraw by the watchful parent each decamps with an egg in its mouth.

These most interesting observations were confirmed by Hippel, who also noticed that half a dozen or more monitors will at once appear on breeding sites whenever the crocodiles have been disturbed

*Monitor lizard*

and driven away. One of the saurians occasionally turns back and
rushes among the marauders, scattering them in all directions, and the
fact that Cott recorded monitor remains from nine crocodile stomachs
indicates that a nest robber now and then has to pay dearly for his
temerity.

The monitor lizards of Australia—known as 'goannas'—also have a
reputation for raiding crocodiles' nests.

Diodorus and other Roman authors credited the ichneumon or
grey mongoose (*Herpestes ichneumon*) with destroying crocodiles'
eggs, and there is no reason why it should not do so. Stevenson-
Hamilton writes of the marsh or water mongoose (*Atilax paludinosus*)
that, together with the monitor, it is 'the most deadly enemy of the
crocodile, scratching out from the sand and devouring its eggs whenever it can do so'.

Spotted hyenas account for quite a number of nests, and so do baboons, warthogs, and bushpigs. Marabou storks have been seen gorging themselves on eggs uncovered by monitors, and vultures, too, can most probably be counted among the nest robbers. A crocodile makes absolutely no effort to repair a damaged nest, and so any interference means the loss of the whole clutch. Wholly or partially exposed eggs are never reburied and will very quickly go rotten in the sun. High temperature can occasionally cause premature hatchings, with the helpless embryos being picked up by scavengers or devoured by ants and maggots.

Incubation is a very lengthy process, lasting for eleven to thirteen weeks in most parts of Africa, and up to fourteen weeks in Zululand. If the clutch escapes the attention of monitors, mongooses and other predators, the eggs eventually begin to swell up, and the hard shell becomes soft and cracks into innumerable fragments. The hatchlings, therefore, have to force their way through the tough inner integument only, and to do this they have a small sharp-pointed piece of lime on the tip of the snout, an egg-tooth, which drops off soon afterwards. The same kind of egg-tooth is also found in birds.

As the time of hatching approaches, baby crocodiles begin to utter croaking sounds, thus inducing the mother to wriggle and squirm around the nest until she has scooped out a roundish, crater-like pit at least down to the uppermost layer of eggs. This is very necessary, for during the long incubation period the soil covering the clutch has hardened considerably, and the hatchlings would find it very difficult, if not impossible, to dig their way up to the surface.

This instinct to help the hatchlings is extremely strong, and the

Illustrations on the following pages:
*Nile crocodile eggs hatching: young crocodile's nose has broken through shell; nose and face breaking through; head is through but front legs still inside egg; with one front leg free, the crocodile heaves to free the other one; shoulders are well out and a final effort frees the crocodile from the egg; minutes after hatching, the crocodile grins contentedly as he basks in the sun*

mother will tackle almost any type of obstacle in order to perform her duty. Pooley writes:

> In December 1967, a hide was built around a nest on the banks of the Pongola River. Stout poles, 15 cm. in diameter, were placed in holes one metre deep around the perimeter of the nest and the poles were firmly tramped down. A fence of No. 8 gauge wire was fitted around the poles, and sacking firmly bound onto the fencing. A roof was made with the same material and in addition, branches and twigs were laid all around the structure. When it was revisited at the estimated hatching time, it was found that the parent had smashed the bottom of the hide, torn away the sacking, and a large excavation revealed that the nest had been opened in the usual manner and the hatchlings released.

While the young are hatching, the mother is in a very aggressive mood, ready to go for any living thing, human or animal, that may happen to make an appearance. An Egyptian who brought Sonnini seven young crocodiles told him that there were about fifty of them together, but that he was unable to catch them all, 'because the mother had arrived unexpectedly and was eager to fly upon him'.

The hatchlings are about 28 cm in length, lively, very agile, and quite capable of giving a human finger a painful nip. Shelford was highly amused to see a yet unhatched saltwater crocodile viciously bite a pencil the moment he took it out of the shell, and the same type of precocious reaction can be expected of a Nile crocodile.

What happens immediately after hatching? The story that the female carries off the young on her back or hanging on to the scales of her tail has so far not been confirmed, but it seems fairly certain that she does escort them to the nearest water, somewhat like a brood of ducklings. There is no reason why the hatchlings, like young turtles, should not find the way by their own instinct, but the mother's presence gives the little creatures a certain amount of protection against the numerous enemies waiting to pounce on them. Adult crocodiles have been seen in shallow water, surrounded by their babies, sometimes even with a few resting on the big animal's back, but the female's interest in her brood is sure to fade away very soon after the young have reached the water.

Hatching takes place at a time when the levels of the rivers are rising, with all the backwaters, inlets, creeks and swamps rapidly filling up, so that there are plenty of places where the baby crocodiles can go. Even though they are very active and can climb into bushes, up trees and even hang on reeds like chameleons, they need every bit of shelter that is available, for they are threatened by innumerable dangers. On land, monitors, marabous, herons, ibis, fish eagles, ravens, eagel owls, ground hornbills and genet cats prey on them from the very moment they leave the nest. In the open water, they become the victims of otters, pelicans, tiger fish, catfish, water turtles (*Trionyx triungis*), hinged terrapins (*Pelusios sinnatus*), and last, but by no means least, of crocodiles. Members of their own species may, in fact, be accounted their worst enemies. On the Ruo River, Blainey Percival once noticed a great commotion among the crocodiles, and as he stalked closer to have a look, he discovered that a nest of crocodiles' eggs was hatching, and as far as he could make out, all the full grown crocodiles in the shallows were snapping up the youngsters just as fast as they reached the water. A few days after having entered this very

*Baby Nile crocodile*

hostile world, baby crocodiles may well be eaten by their own mother, who has just spent so many weeks guarding the nest.

The babies are gregarious immediately after hatching, but they very soon disperse, each one being safest on its own. During the first weeks and months they have nothing to do but to hide as well as they can. There is no need for them to go foraging, for they are well supplied with provisions in the form of a yolk sac about the size of a hen's egg. This is gradually absorbed into the stomach, but a clump of yolk as big as a walnut is still present after eight weeks, and traces of it can be found when the youngsters are six months old. By that time they are already catching insects and other small animals, hunting on land and living very much like lizards. They usually move quite a distance away from the river: along the lower part of the Victoria Nile Cott discovered young crocodiles, about 45 to 53 cm in length, approximately a mile inland in a chain of shallow plant-choked marshes. They were probably 4 to 9 months old.

As time goes by, it becomes increasingly difficult to find any of the youngsters. They are occasionally encountered in the shallows at night, but hardly ever seen in daytime. As Cott put it:

> In areas where, under protection, crocodiles are still abundant, as below Murchison, in the Kafue and Luangwa Reserves, at Mweru wa Ntipa, and Ndumu Reserve in Zululand, the apparent absence of small crocodiles seems the more remarkable. All that one can certainly say is that between the ages of about two and five years, crocodiles go into retreat and since they can have few enemies other than larger individuals of their own kind, it is probable that this cryptic behaviour has been forced upon them by the habit of cannibalism.

From the figures given by Cott, individuals of 2 to 5 years measure from 75 cm to 1.70 metres, and I must admit that I have not very often seen crocodiles between those two sizes. I put up one of about 70 cm on an island below the Murchison Falls frequented by quite a number of adults; when an attempt was made to corner it, the youngster did not, like his elders, escape into the river, but disappeared in fairly thick bush. On another occasion I spotted two specimens of 1 metre or a little less on a tiny island in the Athi River, well below the places where the adults inhabiting the Hippo Pools usually haul out and close to a series of small rapids. In a rather rocky part of the Mara River, with rapids both above and below, I have seen three crocodiles about 1.10 to 1.40 metres in length, and a game scout told me that downriver there were much larger individuals which never came so far up. I also saw one or two fairly small crocodiles immediately below the Lugard Falls in the Tsavo National Park. I would not like to generalise on the basis of so few observations, but I certainly have the impression that crocodiles aged 2–5 years keep out of the way of their elders by hiding in thick undergrowth and in rocky river stretches with rapids and cataracts.

As the crocodiles in Natal have been seen using their hibernation burrows as bolt holes, the question arises whether youngsters might not excavate tunnels of a similar type in order to find safety from predators. So far nobody seems to have recorded such behaviour—but Pooley's observations quite definitely show that the little creatures have an instinct to 'dig for survival'.

In the north-eastern corner of Uganda there is the Kidepo National Park, a dry area of mountains, savannas and bush. The palm-fringed bed of the Kidepo River, from which the park takes its name, is over 100 metres broad in places, but it merely has flash-floods, and water never flows along it for any length of time. The only permanent running water within the park is found in the uppermost parts of the Larus River, which joins the Kidepo across the Sudan border. At the time of my visit, a dam in the Kalabi, one of the tributaries of the Larus, had a couple of medium-sized crocodiles in it, and I could not help wondering whether they had reached their present home one rainy season from the Aswa, making their way up the Kapeta, which has its source in the mountains just outside the park, or had come from somewhere along the Kidepo, far away in the Sudan, where it changes its name to Khor Tug. There was, of course, also the possibility that the crocodiles of the Larus had entered the region at a time when the rivers carried more water and now found themselves cut off from the rest of the crocodilian world.

I was even more puzzled to find five crocodiles in the waterhole of Kananarok, which has a diameter of 15 to 20 metres and owes its existence to a hot spring. Where the water wells out of the ground, it smells strongly of sulphur and must have a temperature of about 40°C, but it quickly loses its warmth and the part inhabited by the saurians is quite cool. The crocodiles I saw in this pool on 2 January 1971 were all small, from 75 cm to about 1 metre, and their heads had the characteristically snubnosed and roundbrowed profile of young animals. Kananarok is roughly 6.5 km from the bed of the Kidepo and 25 km from the upper reaches of the Larus.

The Game Warden of the Kidepo National Park told me that small crocodiles had been seen in the pool for at least four years, and he thought that they had always been the same ones. Their growth may have been somewhat retarded, due to the unsuitability of the habitat. But where did they originally come from? Had they wandered over from the Larus or up the Kidepo in order to escape adult predation? Was the pool of Kananarok perhaps a temporary refuge used by successive generations of youngsters? Crocodiles have provided me with many an interesting observation, many an unforgettable sight, but I have rarely been so thrilled as when I watched the five little ones surfacing for air in the shallow sulphurous pool, in the midst of a landscape where crocodiles are about the last creatures you would expect to come across.

At the Hippo Pools of the Athi River I recently found a crocodile of 2 metres or a little more basking in a place usually occupied by a much larger individual. It had apparently reached a stage in its life when it was no longer simply a prey of larger crocodiles and could show itself openly among its elders, with a good chance of being able to get away without too much trouble in case it should be involved in a territorial contest.

The rate of growth has in the past been very much underestimated. Writing in the early thirties. Pitman quoted an opinion current at that time, which allowed a crocodile an increase of only 1 in per annum during its earlier years. This would give an individual of 2 ft (60 cm) an age of almost 15 years, while a 3 ft (90 cm) specimen could be approaching 30 years.

Growth is, however, not all that slow. From measurements taken on captive crocodiles and on a specimen of undetermined sex which was brought up in a pond in Rhodesia and then released in a natural pan well stocked with catfish and visited by plenty of game animals, it actually appears to be quite rapid during the first seven years, with an average increase of 26.5 to 28 cm per annum, slowing down to a mere 3.6 to 4 cm for the next fifteen years. The growth rate of a young crocodile developing in a habitat where food is plentiful and easily obtainable will, of course, be considerably higher than that of a specimen of equal age that has the misfortune of finding itself in a particularly poor environment.

Individuals of 4 metres and more show a very impressive increase in bulk, and one might almost say that a time comes when they gain more in width than in length. I have had various occasions to compare two basking crocodiles that did not differ very much in their nose-to-tail measurements, but the somewhat longer one had more than twice the girth of its slim companion.

Males have been found to reach sexual maturity when they are about 2.90 to 3.30 metres in length, and have a weight of 80 to 160 kg. Of the females more than half begin to breed after attaining a length of 3 metres and a weight of 120 kg, and only very few breed before measuring at least 2.44 metres. The smallest breeding females recorded from Lake Victoria had a length of 2.18 to 2.33 metres.

In trying to correlate the sizes and weights of crocodiles in breeding condition with what had become known with respect to the growth rate of these reptiles, Cott noticed discrepancies that seemed to point to males growing more rapidly than females. He eventually came to the conclusion that female Nile crocodiles did not reach maturity before the age of about ten years.

A difference in the male and female growth rate has, in fact, been definitely proved for the American alligator. During the first four or five years, males and females annually add about 30 cm to their length. Males maintain this rate till the seventh year, while females begin to grow more slowly from the fourth or fifth year onward. At six years the difference in size between males and females of equal ages is already very noticeable and can be just over half a metre in the tenth year. A minimal breeding age of 9 years and 10 months has been recorded for a female of 2.21 metres.

Alligators mate in May and early June. The female then looks for a dry sunny spot close to the water, but she does not dig a pit like the Nile crocodile; not having the tropical sun to warm up the soil, she has to provide herself with an incubator. She uses her broad jaws to scoop up mud which she mixes with mouthfuls of vegetable matter and then builds a mound about 1 metre high and 2 metres across. She shapes and smoothes this structure by crawling over and round it and digs a hollow in the top, into which she deposits her 20 to 70 eggs in two tiers. She closes the opening with material from the rim, levels out the top of the mound, and there is her incubator, finished and operational, with the eggs embedded in a constantly humid environment and the processes of fermentation generating a temperature always somewhat above that of the outside.

The female alligator remains on guard until the babies hatch after an incubation period of about nine weeks. As soon as she hears their peeping calls, she tears open the mound, releases the hatchlings and leads them to the nearest water. When emerging from the eggs, baby alligators have a length of about 20 cm.

Caimans belong to the American tropics, but they entrust their eggs to incubators like the alligator. One might think that there would be plenty of sun and heat, but very many of the rivers they inhabit run through vast forests of great density, and the saurians often have to build their nests in the deepest shade. The nesting mounds of the Spectacled and Black caimans living in forest areas consist of fallen leaves. Where the jacaré-açu—the Black caiman—breeds in more open savanna-like country, the female scratches together broken and trampled reeds, and the resulting mound, about 80 cm high and 1.50 metres across, can be likened to a small haystack. The 30 to 50 eggs are embedded about 40 cm above ground. The mother guards the nest and keeps the mound humid, and she is said to look after the freshly hatched young and to defend them against enemies.

The two West African species—the Long-snouted and the Broad-fronted crocodiles—occur in forest streams, and they both deposit their eggs in piles of rotten vegetation. Cansdale writes of the Broad-fronted crocodile:

> It seems probable that no more than a dozen or so eggs are laid at a time, but this is another of the very many things about West African crocodiles which are still unknown. Up to about a dozen newly hatched young might be found together, and it seems that the mother guards them for a time after they are hatched.

The Estuarine crocodile, which often breeds in coastal and riverain jungles and forests, also makes use of an incubator. The female goes to a damp and secluded spot and rakes dead leaves and rushes into a mound that may have a circumference of 9 metres and stand about 90 cm high in the centre. The eggs, 40 to 60 in number, are buried about 60 cm from the top. The warmth generated by the decomposing vegetation is described as quite astonishing, and it increases the farther one digs into the mound. According to reports both from Malaya and Australia, the mother scoops out a wallow near the nest in which she settles down to guard her clutch. She keeps the mound humid by splashing water over it with her tail.

Charles Hose of Sarawak fame was attacked with great fury when he attempted to examine a nest of this species. A huge crocodile suddenly came up just beneath the bow of his boat and rose out of the water, one foot on the gunwale, the other on a palm stump. Hose grabbed a pole and pushed it between the wide open jaws gaping at him, while the two boatmen began hacking at the saurian. The little craft was just about to capsize, when the crocodile suddenly sank back and disappeared.

It is possible that nests of the Estuarine crocodile are not always of exactly the same type. Dahl describes old nests in the dry savanna country of Arnhem Land as small scattered hillocks of sand, where old eggshells were plentiful; while Shelford, in his account of the saltwater crocodile's breeding habits in Borneo, writes that the 30 to 40 eggs are deposited in a depression the female makes in the sand, among the stems of Nipa-palms, usually at a little distance from the water.

The breeding habits of the mugger are much like those of the Nile crocodile and similarly regulated by the seasons. In Central India Dunbar Brander took mature eggs, usually about 30 in number, from females at the beginning of the hot weather and saw newly hatched young after the rains had started. The female selects a site with sandy soil close to some brushwood or palm grove, scoops out a pit about 50 cm deep and deposits her eggs in layers. She spends most of the incubation period practically on top of the nest.

The gavial, too, buries its 40 eggs in the sand, in two tiers separated from each other by a fairly thick layer of sand. The hatchlings have a length of 40 cm, of which 4 cm are taken up by the muzzle and 22 cm by the tail.

The tremendous toll of baby crocodiles taken by various predators has already been mentioned, and considering the large size of the clutches it can certainly be said that of all the crocodiles hatched out only a very small percentage survive long enough to attain a length of 1.70 metres. Stevenson-Hamilton put the survival rate at 1 per cent, and this may not be far out. Pooley tells of placing 114 newly hatched crocodiles in a small stream flowing into a pan swarming with hammerkops, openbill storks, wood ibis, yellow billed kites, pied crows and white pelicans. After a period of three weeks not a single crocodile could be found, despite a prolonged search among reedbeds and other sheltered areas, both by day and by night. Pooley wrote:

> Twenty tagged crocodiles between 45 cm. and 60 cm. in length were released into the same pan on 12th July 1967. A flock of white pelicans, estimated at 500, arrived the same day. Subsequent visits to the pan at night and by day, showed how rapidly those crocodiles had disappeared. After seven days only 3 could be found, after one month 2 remained, and after three months only 1 out of the twenty could be found. In addition to the birds mentioned, the population of adult crocodiles was high and monitor lizards were frequently noted.

Genet cats took several crocodiles aged about 3 months from the pools of the hatchery, and a pair of spotted eagle owls developed a great predilection for the little saurians, paying nightly visits to the pools. A fish eagle was seen to catch a crocodile about 82 cm in length and to carry it away without any difficulty.

The heavy predation on the young is the controlling mechanism that keeps the numbers of crocodiles in check and prevents the tropical waters from becoming overcrowded with them. Once a crocodile has grown to a length of 2 metres and more, it is almost invulnerable, or would be if it were not for man's modern hunting methods.

Nature does not produce absolute invulnerability, and a certain number of crocodiles are, of course, killed or badly incapacitated later in life, but these losses are too insignificant to have a controlling effect. The greatest threat to adult crocodiles probably comes from the fights they have among themselves—the mating battles and the territorial contests for basking grounds and feeding places. I have seen several individuals that had lost considerable portions of their tails, and Cott gives a long list of injuries he noticed in the specimens he had shot and examined.

That damage of a much more serious nature can be inflicted was shown by 'Old Mose', the alligator of the New York Zoological Park, when he suddenly seized an 8 ft companion, lifted him right out of the water and shook him with such vehemence that the skin of the back was torn in two. In another encounter, one of the alligators grabbed the opponent's leg and, setting itself into rotating motion, twisted it off in 5 seconds. Hornaday once shot a very emaciated alligator that had half its upper jaw bitten off. It was the only one he ever saw lift its body off the ground and run on four legs. Some mention will later be made of the near-fatal wounds 'Lutembe', Uganda's most famous crocodile, received in a fight that was probably of a territorial nature.

Hippos and elephants occasionally kill crocodiles, but incidents of this kind can be considered as coming under the heading of 'accidental death'. In the Luangwa Valley a leopard once managed to get the better of a crocodile wandering overland from one pan to another, but while 'spots' may take quite a number of youngsters, the lion is probably the only African animal that can be said really to prey on adults. This seems to happen not infrequently along Lake Rudolf and on the Lake Albert flats of Uganda, and it has also been recorded from the Victoria Nile.

There exists an often reproduced photograph showing a tiger in the act of grabbing a crocodile in shallow water. It is an agency picture, and I do not know by whom it was originally taken. It could be the kind of fabulously lucky shot all animal photographers dream about, but it somehow reminds me of bogus jungle films of the *Bring 'Em Back Alive* and *Wild Cargo* type, which were so popular in the 1930s. I should not be surprised one day to hear that the tiger had been baited with a dead crocodile, or that the whole 'encounter' was staged in an enclosure. The photograph does, however, show a scene that must have taken place on a good number of occasions, specially in the Sunderbans, where both tigers and crocodiles were common in former times.

An authentic account of an incident very similar to the one depicted on the old photograph is given by Henry Walter Bates, the feline predator in this case not being the Asian tiger but the jaguar, known as 'el tigre' over most of South and Central America. Bates writes:

After walking half a mile, we came upon a dry watercourse, where we observed, first the old footmarks of a tapir, and, soon after on the margin of a curious circular hole full of muddy water, the first track of a jaguar. This latter discovery was hardly made when a rush was heard amidst the bushes on the top of the sloping bank on the opposite side of the dried creek. We bounded forward, it was, however, too late for the animal had sped in a few moments far out of our reach. It was clear we had disturbed, on our approach, the jaguar whilst quenching his thirst at the water hole. A few steps farther on we saw the mangled remains of an alligator (the Jacaré tinga).

The head, forequarters and bony shell were the only parts which remained, but the meat was quite fresh, and there were many footmarks of the jaguar around the carcass, so that there was no doubt this had formed the solid part of the animal's breakfast. My companions now began to search for the alligator's nest, the presence of the reptile so far from the river being accountable for on no other ground than the maternal solicitude for its eggs. We found, in fact, the nest at the distance of a few yards from the place. It was a conical pile of dead leaves, in the middle of which twenty eggs were buried.

The jaguar had stalked the Spectacled caiman as it was guarding the nest, and it seems more than likely that muggers, Estuarine crocodiles and Nile crocodiles have been killed by tigers and lions under exactly the same circumstances. But even though predation on adults by large felines does occur, it is certainly not on a scale which would make it a factor limiting crocodile populations.

Hans Krieg frequently saw the Spectacled caimans of the Gran Chaco preying upon those most terrifying inhabitants of South American waters, the piranhas. They caught them easily and in great numbers, for the backwaters were literally swarming with the voracious fish. On one occasion, having shot a caiman, Krieg watched the piranhas feeding on the carcase. In no time the water was boiling with fish, but this soon attracted other caimans who now went to work snapping up the cannibal fish as fast as they could. It gave Krieg no little satisfaction to see the piranhas for once getting the worst of a bargain.

Under normal circumstances caimans are quite obviously not molested by the fish. Things change, however, as soon as one of the saurians gets wounded, and the piranhas are then able to take their revenge. When Theodore Roosevelt descended the Rio Duvida— the 'River of Doubt', now the Rio Theodore Roosevelt—a 5 ft caiman wounded by a shot was immediately attacked and actually driven out of the water to face his human enemies. 'The fish first attacked the wound, then, as the blood maddened them, they attacked all the soft parts, their terrible teeth cutting out chunks of tough hide and flesh,' wrote Roosevelt, describing the scene. This observation has been confirmed by Hans Krieg and by many other naturalists. Travelling up the Rio Ucayali, Kenneth Vinton and other passengers repeatedly fired at the numerous caimans, and it was noticed that upon being hit, many of them hurridly made for the river bank. When Vinton remarked upon this strange behaviour, an old Amazon trader said: 'The answer is simple. When your bullets draw blood, the piranhas begin biting him, so he hurries out on the playa to escape them'.

The Marquis de Wavrin had good evidence of caimans occasionally being killed and eaten by large anacondas.

On 28 April 1903, Sir David Bruce and the members of a Royal Society Commission, who had all come to Uganda to investigate an epidemic with a truly appalling mortality rate, announced that the disease, known popularly as sleeping sickness, was caused by a trypanosome—later identified as *Trypanosoma gambiense*—which parasite was carried from man to man by the tsetse fly, *Glossina palpalis*. From then onward, research into the bionomics of tsetse flies centred on the Lake Victoria area, and it was soon realised that these biting insects actually preferred the blood of crocodiles and monitors to that of humans. Taking into consideration the crocodiles' scaly armour one would have thought it difficult for the tsetse fly to pierce it, but this is not so. Hale-Carpenter one day tethered a small crocodile near the water, watched it closely from 8.35 to 9.45 am and counted forty flies feeding on it to repletion, mostly on the eyelids, the hindlegs and the neck. Anybody who has had an opportunity to watch crocodiles from a fairly short distance with a good pair of binoculars will have noticed tsetse flies settling on adults as well.

*Glossina palpalis* not only carries *Trypanosoma gambiense*, but also two crocodile blood-parasites, *Trypanosoma grayi*, which is harmless to man, and a haemagregarine, *Hepatozoon petiti*. We do not know whether these parasites are in any way injurious to the reptiles, but their effect cannot be very serious, nor that of the nematodes that have been found as intestinal parasites in crocodiles' stomachs. The leeches, with which they can be infested fairly heavily, may be a nuisance, but they, too, do not harm a crocodile to such a degree as to shorten its life.

Among a dozen muggers Hornaday obtained from a rather overcrowded pool in Ceylon, two 7 ft specimens were afflicted with a cutaneous disease that looked somewhat like a form of leprosy. Hornaday gives the following description of it:

In one, the whole left side of the head, the neck and throat were the parts affected, and in the other it was the entire tail. On these parts the epidermis had peeled off entirely, and the skin was covered with huge scale-like scabs, which, when peeled off, left the diseased skin of an unwholesome, bluish colour. Both specimens had running sores at the points where the sternum and the pelvis touched the ground, and both were so emaciated as to be little more than skin and bone. In the stomach of one I found a handful of swamp grass and a lot of small pebbles.

No similar disease is mentioned from any part of Africa. Owen, with a considerable experience of crocodiles in the Sudan, explicitly states that he did not come across any evidence of epidemic diseases.

Before modern hunters appeared on the scene, a crocodile that had managed to survive until it reached maturity would have been a very good insurance risk, for it had excellent prospects of living for a long time. It is, of course, easy to say 'a long time', but what does it really mean? What would be the life expectancy of a crocodile in a world without professional hunters and poachers?

Various crocodilians exhibited by showmen have been introduced to the public as having lived for hundreds or even for thousands of years. Such claims are unsubstantiated and cannot be taken seriously, but zoological gardens have provided us with plenty of reliable data. An American alligator in Dresden is known to have attained an age of at least 56 years, and many other representatives of this species lived for over 30 years. A Chinese alligator in Berlin reached 50 years, a mugger in Trivandrum 31 years, a gavial in London 28 years and 9 months, and a Nile crocodile in Berlin 25 years. While mammals and birds tend to live longer in captivity than under natural conditions, reptiles seem to be adversely affected by confinement, so that the figures given above can be considered as being rather low. Cott tells us that the Nile crocodile kept under observation in Rhodesia was still growing at the age of 22 years, and he goes on to say:

> If growth after 22 years continues at the rate indicated in Davison's field measurements, at about 1.4 inches per annum, then a crocodile measuring 15 feet in length would be about 76 years old, and one measuring 18 feet would be over 100 years old. But if, as is most likely, the growth curve flattens out in late life, then the largest known specimens must have survived well into their second century.

It is a great pity that we do not know more about the life story of 'Lutembe', a crocodile that for a long time resided in a small bay of the Murchison Gulf in Lake Victoria and usually came out to be fed with fish when called by name. If it did not show up at once, the fishermen used to beat the water with paddles, and this rarely failed to bring the saurian to the shore. 'Lutembe' became world-famous during the mid-twenties, when Cherry Kearton made it the star of his animal film *Tembi*, which, as a schoolboy, I sat through not once but at least half a dozen times. Judging from the photographs published in several of Cherry Kearton's books, the animal, which the locals always declared to be a female, was then a big crocodile, though nothing out of the ordinary in its proportions. Murray Smith estimated its length at about 14 ft (4.25 metres). 'Lutembe' turned into a tourist attraction long before tourism became one of East Africa's major industries, and for many years it must have been one of the most photographed animals in the world.

How old was 'Lutembe' at the time of its—or perhaps rather her—debut in front of Cherry Kearton's camera? Pitman, who knew the lady very well, wrote in 1931 that the origin of her association with the fishermen of Murchison Gulf was unknown, though she had apparently been an object of veneration for a long time. That is most probably all that can be said without entering the realms of speculation and fantasy. There certainly were very sinister rumours concerning 'Lutembe's' past, and they have on more than one occasion been stated as facts. It was claimed that the famous crocodile had started her career as a royal executioner, devouring the poor wretches that had had the misfortune to draw upon their heads the wrath of one or other of the nineteenth-century kings of Uganda. We shall see that there have been instances of crocodiles performing such functions, but nothing can be found in the writings of explorers and pioneer missionaries to substantiate 'Lutembe's' connection with them. While this clears 'Lutembe's' character, however, it also prevents us from fixing a date to some point of her past life.

Pitman carried on the 'Lutembe' story in 1942, when he wrote:

> In recent years Uganda's 'pet' crocodile 'Lutembe' has begun to show un-mistakable signs of senility. Nowadays, oblivious of the proximity of onlookers, she often refuses to return to her watery home after a good feed and falls asleep on the shore, her hideous features set in a most bestial expression. There she will lie for hours at a time. For several years 'Lutembe's' foster folk, with an eye to the future, in the event of any evil day befalling their protegé, have been trying to encourage other crocodiles to partake of the hospitality of strangers. The motive, of course, is scarcely philanthropic, for with the departure of 'Lutembe' an ever-increasing source of revenue would disappear. As far back as 1933 a slightly smaller example would occasionally answer the custodian's call, that is, when 'Lutembe' was not

about, for she at once demonstrated in no uncertain fashion what she was prepared to do to intruders of her species who had the temerity to poach on her preserves. But old age creepeth on and 'Lutembe' is no longer in control of the situation. In fact, at the end of 1937 she all but brought her life to a close in a mortal combat with another. For a time she was in a sorry plight and for many months displayed prominently terrible wounds. Eventually she recovered. If a crocodile can ever look pathetic, 'Lutembe', from all accounts, certainly looked it during this period of crisis and curiously enough did return to her human associates to die or be cured. She lay on the shore for a fortnight, scarcely moving. Her guardians were convinced she would die. No longer in undisputed possession of her lucrative beat, it is now possible to witness the remarkable sight of two entirely wild crocodiles asleep peacefully on the shore with the local villagers washing clothes only a few paces from them. The newcomer which one day I watched being fed at the same time as the old and decrepit 'Lutembe', was most bold and active.

I shall always regret that I did not meet the lady whom I had admired on the silent screen in my younger days. 'Lutembe' disappeared during the 1940s, and we shall never know whether she fought another and this time fatal battle, or simply died of old age, as even a crocodile eventually must.

# 6. Man-eating Crocodiles

One of Baker's men seized by a crocodile (*Baker: Ismailia*)

THE darkly opaque waters of the Nianam River—also known as the Omo—were slowly flowing south towards Lake Rudolf, named only ten years earlier by the explorers Teleki and von Hoehnel. A white man looked out across the unruffled surface to where the sun was already standing low over the western horizon. He was Arthur H. Neumann, the English big-game hunter, and he had arrived at the large fenced village of Kere that very day. A short while ago, he had suddenly remembered that it was New Year's Day, 1896. Well, within hundreds of miles there was no man of his own race with whom he could have celebrated. He was, in fact, the first European to have seen Lake Rudolf after Teleki and von Hoehnel, and they had not come as far up the Omo as Kere. Neumann went down to the river to have a bath, followed by Shebane, his Swahili servant, who carried his chair and towels. Some crocodiles had earlier been seen in the middle of the river, but for months Neumann and his men had been bathing right among these saurians in Lake Rudolf without being harmed in any way, and they had gradually come to disregard them altogether.

Having performed his ablutions and put on his clothes, the hunter sat down in his chair with the back to the setting sun, and began lacing his boots. He noticed that Shebane had undressed to wash himself, but did not pay any attention to the servant until he heard a cry of alarm. Looking up, Neumann got a glimpse of the most ghastly scene he had ever seen—for there was Shebane, held across the middle of his body in the jaws of a huge crocodile, like a fish in a heron's beak. The reptile was just swinging round towards the deep water, and before Neumann could even move, there was a swirl, a splash, and the crocodile had disappeared, taking along its unfortunate victim. Some of Neumann's men had witnessed the tragedy and came running down the steep bank with guns. But nothing could be done to save poor faithful Shebane. A malancholy termination to a New Year's Day!

The expedition which Sir Samuel Baker took up the Nile on behalf of the Egyptian Government, seven years after discovering Lake Albert and the Murchison Falls, consisted of a whole fleet of ships and hundreds of men, most of them quite unacquainted with the dangers that awaited them in the southern Sudan. Consequently there were many distressing losses through crocodiles. On one occasion a servant sat upon the deck of one of the deeply laden vessels, with his legs dangling over the sides, the feet half a yard above the water. There was a sudden rush, a large crocodile seized the man and carried him off in the presence of 100 men who were quite unable to come to his rescue. Baker wrote:

> Among the accidents that occurred to my expedition, one man had his arm bitten off at the elbow, being seized while collecting aquatic vegetation from the bank. He was saved from utter loss by his comrades who held him while his arm was in the jaws of the crocodile. The man was brought to me in dreadful agony, and the stump was immediately amputated above the fracture. Another man was seized by the leg while assisting to push a vessel off a sandbank. He also was saved by a crowd of soldiers who were with him engaged on the same work; this man lost his leg. The captain of No. 10 tug

*Crocodile returning to the water in Murchison Falls National Park, Uganda*

was drowned in the dock vacated by the 108 ton steamer, which had been floated into the river by a small canal cut from the basin for that purpose. The channel was about 30 yards in length and 3 feet in depth. No person ever suspected that a crocodile would take possession of the dock, and it was considered the safest place for the troops to bathe. One evening, at muster the captain was absent and as it was known that a short time previously he had gone down to wash at the basin, he was searched for at the place. A pile of clothes and his red fez were upon the bank, but no person was visible. A number of men jumped into the water, and felt the bottom in every portion of the dock, with the result that in a few minutes his body was discovered; one leg was broken in several places, being severely mangled by the numerous teeth of the crocodile. There can be little doubt that the creature, having drowned its victim, had intended to return.

Some months after this incident, a terrible calamity in the same canal was adjudged to have been occasioned by the same crocodile, although no actual proof could be adduced. About 7 p.m., Lady Baker and myself, together with Commander Julian Baker, R.N., were sitting in an open shed in the comparative cool of evening, when a man rushed past the sentries and threw himself upon the ground, clasping my legs in an agony of terrified excitement. The sentries immediately rushed forward and seized him by the back of the neck. Releasing him instantly by my order, the man gasped out, 'Said, Said is gone! Taken away from my side by a crocodile, now, this minute!'—'Said! What Said?' I asked: 'There are many Saids'—'Said of the No. 10 steamer, the man you liked, he is gone, we were wading together across the canal by the dock where Reis Mahomet was killed, the water is only waist deep, but a tremendous crocodile rushed like a steamer from the river, seized Said by the waist and disappeared. He's dragged into the river, and I've run here to tell you the bad news.' We immediately hurried to the spot. The surface of the river was calm and unruffled in the stillness of a fine night. The canal was quiet, and appeared as though it had never been disturbed. The man who had lost his companion sat down and sniffed aloud. Said, who was one of my best men, was indeed gone for ever.

A book could easily be filled with harrowing tales of this kind, not only from the heroic age of African exploration but also of much more recent occurrence. Many people from Europe and America today visit the Mzima Springs in Tsavo National Park, those crystal clear basins in the midst of a semi-desert landscape, surrounded by palm trees and reeds, inhabited by a considerable herd of hippopotami. A number of years ago, before the spot became a tourist attraction, a European family from Nairobi went to the springs for a picnic. There are plenty of elephants and rhinos in the area, not to speak of the possibility that a lion or leopard might be lurking near the water, and it seems quite incredible that the parents ever let the children, a boy and a girl, get out of sight. But this they did, and while playing about in one of the pools, the girl was horrified to see a crocodile rush out of a papyrus thicket, grab her brother and drag him away! Screaming for help she ran back to her parents who immediately started out to search for the boy, assisted by the game scouts stationed at the springs. It took hours to find the body, which had been hidden away in the middle of a dense bed of reeds.

Stevenson-Hamilton tells of a Bantu youth who was taken when fetching water from a pool in the bed of the Sabi River. The villagers waded into the water, searching the bottom of the pool with their spears, and they eventually found the corpse, with only a few tooth marks, in a cavity under the river bank. There have been reports from various parts of Africa of people who, having lost consciousness while being dragged under water came to in such a cavern and managed to scramble out of it or to dig a passage up to the surface. Some of these stories might well be true.

Most human victims are taken on the very edge of the river or lake, when they come down to draw water, to bathe or wash their clothes. As far as a crocodile on the look-out for mammalian prey is concerned, there is, of course, absolutely no difference between a woman bending down to fill her calabash and an antelope lowering its muzzle for a drink of water. Both are fair game to the cruising or lurking saurian, and both are exposing themselves to its attack in exactly the same way. The crocodile simply reacts to the opportunity that presents itself as his ancestors have been doing for untold ages.

People wading across rivers are sometimes seized, though a lot of noise, for instance a few shots fired into the water, will usually scare crocodiles away from a ford. There is, in this case, much to be said for 'safety in numbers', for while a man entering a crocodile-infested pool or river on his own might be taken, the timid reptiles will hardly ever approach a crowd. There have been occasional attacks upon canoes and boats, with attempts to throw a man sitting on the gunwale into the water or to grab one of the persons on board. Mary Kingsley heard of several natives losing their lives in this way, and she herself, when tide-trapped in a swampy lagoon, had to fight off an 8 ft saurian that put its forefeet on the stern of her canoe. But let the lady explorer describe this encounter in her own inimitable style: 'I had to retire to the bows to keep the balance—it is no use saying because I was frightened, for this miserably understates the case—and fetch him a clip on the snout with the paddle, when he withdrew, and I paddled into the middle of the lagoon, hoping the water there was too deep for him or any of his friends to repeat the performance'.

Going up the Zambezi in a small aluminium launch, Major A. St H. Gibbons was standing at the helm, in order to command as wide a field of vision as possible and working the tiller with his feet, when he suddenly noticed a submerged object approaching at a great pace. Next moment a crocodile hit the boat just below his feet, and so forceful was the impact that Gibbons very nearly lost his balance, and the people in the forward part of the launch thought that she had struck a rock.

Attacks on boats may sometimes have been due to an error on the part of the crocodile: at least, that was the only explanation Stanley could find for the behaviour of a big crocodile which, in the early days of the Congo Freestate, rushed at the wheel of his little steamboat and was trying to catch hold of it when a well placed bullet saved the fragile mechanism from serious damage. The reptile probably mistook the flapping paddles for the limbs of a swimming animal.

In Barotseland Gibbons once heard of a crocodile that entered a hut at night, grabbed a sleeping man and dragged him into the river. Similar occurrences have been reported from the Juba River and from other parts of Africa.

A most horrifying story came from a medical officer travelling on the Congo. At a point where the steamer had to move slowly in order to negotiate some sandbanks, he found himself watching a young man rowing across the river. All at once he noticed a crocodile that was obviously following in the wake of the canoe. The solitary boatman realised his danger and began paddling for all he was worth. The crocodile surged forward like a battle cruiser, but just as it was beginning to overtake the canoe, the man succeeded in beaching his small craft on a little island. The people on board the steamer heaved a sigh of relief when they saw him jump ashore and run away from the water, but the crocodile walked straight out of the river and ran after the youth, who soon reached the end of the island and doubled back in terror. As nobody had a rifle handy, the spectators had to watch helplessly as the saurian knocked him down with its tail, and carried him off into the river. There are, of course, well authenticated cases of animals having been killed on land, and looked at in this light the action of this saurian may not be all that extraordinary.

Certain places have acquired an especially bad reputation for man-eating crocodiles. One was the lower Pongola River, the murky waters of which gave the reptiles good cover and made things easy for them. Another was the Juba River, where crocodiles were so 'rapacious and enterprising' that the people along its course were afraid to approach the water, except where there were steep banks.

Sesheke on the Zambezi was reputed to be a sinister spot, though the fault there lay more with the humans than with the reptiles. The town had at one time been the residence of a king of the Barotse named Sepopo, who took great pleasure in having large numbers of people executed for witchcraft and other imagined offences. The victims were thrown into the river and eaten by the crocodiles. Sepopo came to an unpleasant end himself, through assassination, in 1870, yet when Gibbons visited Sesheke in 1895 man-eating crocodiles were still unusually common.

It has often been stated that crocodiles kill many more humans than lions and leopards do, and this may have been true in times not so far back, when the saurians were still very common in African waters. There has, however, always been a strange difference in the way the natives reacted to the occasional threat from big cats and to the constant danger from crocodiles. The appearance of a man-eating lion is even today a terrifying event that causes widespread apprehension and sometimes even panic. Everybody is keenly aware of the peril lurking in the bush, and the villagers make certain not to be overtaken by darkness away from the comparative safety of their huts. The men band together in an effort to destroy the marauder, or ask for help from the game department if they do not feel capable of dealing with the emergency. When it comes to crocodiles, however, these same people usually display a quite amazing indifference, and it is rare for even the most elementary precautions to be taken.

Monteiro did see places staked round on the banks of Angolan rivers to enable people to fill their vessels without danger, and Fonck reported villages on the Malagarasy where palisades had been built along the river front, and the women drew water by means of calabashes fastened to long poles, but such attempts at reducing the depredations by crocodiles have always been exceptional. Innumerable stories illustrating the general disregard of the danger lurking in the water have been recorded.

For one, a hunter shot a hippo, and his men spent the afternoon cutting up the dead animal. The blood running into the water and the smell, which under the tropical sun rapidly became more and more penetrating, attracted a few crocodiles. They took up position some distance away, patiently watching and waiting. At sunset a number of women and children came wading out into the shallows and proceeded to fill their water containers halfway between the hippo carcase and the crocodiles.

For another, at St Lucia Bay a Zulu jumped into a channel well known to contain numbers of crocodiles in order to push a pontoon away from the bank. A flurry, a swirl—and he was gone, never to be seen again. The following day several Zulus were seen swimming across that same channel as if nothing had happened.

Thirdly, a woman washing her baby on the shore of Lake Albert paid absolutely no attention to a large crocodile that slowly swam past about 20 metres away. A European shouted a warning—but she called back that crocodiles did not eat people.

Well could Murray Smith write: 'The surprise is that not so many but that so few Africans are killed, for these careless people take the most appalling risks'.

To a certain degree it may be a case of familiarity breeding contempt. A man-eating lion is certainly not an every-day phenomenon, and he roams around at night, unseen and mysterious, covering quite a large area and striking now here, now there. Nobody ever knows exactly where he is or where he will turn up next. The crocodiles, however, are always out there in the river, as they have been for generations. Everybody has seen them and knows that most of them will not attack humans. So, why worry? Africans have a good deal of fatalism, and if an accident does happen, they tend to say: 'Haizuru—shauri ya mungu! —Never mind—it was God's will!' We shall see that this apparent indifference can sometimes be the result of superstitious beliefs.

There is no denying that numbers of people have been killed by Nile crocodiles, but it can also be said that the actual death toll has often been greatly exaggerated. I have, for instance, seen it quite seriously assessed at 20,000 persons a year. This figure was admittedly meant to refer to conditions as they were thirty or forty years ago, but even for that time it can only be regarded as absurd, and James Clarke must surely be much nearer the mark in putting it at about

3,000 deaths per annum. The truth is that we simply do not know, and that there are no statistics to help us. Certain considerations make it likely, however, that even Clarke's figure could be too high.

It must be kept in mind that within a given population of Nile crocodiles the majority are predominantly fish-eaters. While small mammals are taken by all age groups, large mammals only begin to have a certain importance for crocodiles ranging from 3 to 5 metres. If you should carelessly enter a river near the place where a crocodile of over 3 metres is lying, or if you happen to fall out of your canoe close to it, you do, of course, run a certain risk. In most places the formidable looking saurians are really very shy, and your sudden appearance or the splash of your fall may quite well scare the animal away. We also know that crocodiles are by no means voracious and constant feeders, and there is a fair chance of your particular individual not being ready for a meal. It may, on the other hand, rush at you in the normal and quite automatic reaction of a hungry predator in the presence of an unexpected prey. Such attacks must be considered as more or less accidental, and it is certainly significant that of all the hundreds of stomachs examined by Cott and his collaborators only four—two from the Kafue, one from the Zambezi and one from Zululand—should have contained human remains. We cannot even be quite certain that all these crocodiles really did kill humans; being great scavengers, they would naturally feed on the corpse of a drowned man.

Confirmed man-eaters are mostly very big animals, clumsy with old age, which have come to realise that humans not only tend to come regularly to certain places along the river, but can also be caught more easily than any other mammalian prey. Such animals do cause much harm, but it is not necessary to exaggerate their depredations. A professional crocodile hunter has credited two of these monsters with 400 and 300 human victims respectively, but these figures were quite unsubstantiated and were probably only used to justify the mass slaughter of crocodiles that has been going on for much too long.

In Ghana, according to Cansdale, it is rare to hear of anybody injured by a crocodile. 'The only authentic case which came to my notice,' he writes, 'was of a European who was caught by the leg while on training exercise in northern Ashanti during the war. He was rescued and survived more or less intact. There must be other cases but I found them hard to check'.

Just as there are—or were—'black spots', certain areas have acquired fame for the exemplary behaviour of their crocodiles. Stevenson-Hamilton mentions some large pans in Amatongaland, which, though full of crocodiles, were considered as perfectly safe for bathing, no attack ever having been reported. Lake Baringo in Kenya, a place of which I have some personal experience, has long enjoyed a similar reputation. The inoffensive disposition of the Baringo crocodiles was, I think, first pointed out by Major P. H. G. Powell-Cotton, who referred to them as by far the most mild mannered crocodiles he had come across either in Africa or Asia. He thought that their amicable ways were due to the lake literally swarming with fish.

I was lucky enough to see Baringo before a professional crocodile hunter had established himself on its shore. The big reptiles were at that time very numerous indeed, and their scaly backs could continually be seen crossing and recrossing the surface of the lake. I had read the accounts given by Powell-Cotton and others, but I was still surprised at the sight of Kamasia tribesmen standing up to their armpits in the water as they were fishing for tilapia quite far from land, with crocodiles swimming past at no great distance.

'Are you not afraid of the "mamba"—the crocodiles?' I asked one of the fishermen, as he came wading out of the lake with his catch.

He laughed and said: 'Why should I be afraid of them Bwana? They are not "kali" (vicious). If we step on one of them it rushes off very quickly'.

Another Kamasia added: 'The "mamba" of Baringo are not like those of Kisumu on the Nyanza (Lake Victoria). There they will eat people, but here they do no harm'.

I kept on questioning the locals, but the answer was always the same, and there could be no shadow of a doubt that the Baringo crocodiles were inoffensive. I had myself rowed out in, or rather on, one of the Ambatch canoes that were then in general use on the lake. These canoes were somewhat boat-shaped bundles of sticks (one sat as much in as out of the water) propelled by two very short paddles which the boatman slipped over his hands almost like a pair of gloves. Nothing could be easier for a crocodile than to pluck a man off such a craft, but the reptiles took absolutely no notice of us.

In Madagascar, too, there are certain areas where humans seem to be immune from attacks. The description Decary gives of people fishing among crocodiles in the little lakes of the Mananarakaka Valley certainly brings to mind Lake Baringo.

James Clarke thinks that even today at least 1,000 lives a year are lost through crocodiles in the whole of Africa, with about the same number being injured in abortive attacks. We still have no reliable statistics to draw upon, and any figure given can only be regarded as a guess. Crocodiles have, however, become very rare in most of their haunts, so that the number of fatalities may be much less than Clarke's not unreasonable assessment. The reptiles are not infrequently accused of killings for which they are not responsible. A couple of months ago a tourist taking photographs of the Lugard Falls slipped on the rocks and fell into the Galana River. He was swept away by the current, never to be seen again, and the story went round that he had been snapped up by a crocodile. Nobody saw this happen, and the most likely assumption is that the unfortunate man was drowned, though the body may later have been found by a crocodile.

Something about the big saurians has always inspired the telling of tall tales, like the one of the crocodile that grabbed the first man in a chain-gang of convicts and then pulled all the unfortunate wretches into the water, gobbling them up one by one. It is a famous African story that from time to time turns up in various parts of the continent. It was, in fact, once told to Richard Hakluyt by Andrew Battell, the sixteenth-century sailor who spent eighteen years among the Portuguese in Angola! One wonders how long it had been going around before that. Did Roman officers and administrators returning from Egypt tell it to amuse their stay-at-home friends?

Similar stories have, however, been invented in much more recent times. About twenty-five years ago there was a certain vogue for African books of, to put it mildly, a very 'adventurous' character, with crocodiles usually playing quite a prominent part. I can remember a hilariously fantastic account of a 'mass migration' of thousands of crocodiles, which, coming out of the Zambezi in serried ranks, threatened to overwhelm the author's camp. Another traveller described his arrival in a village where he was told of a bad old croco-dile in the nearby river that had, in the course of several decades, consumed a missionary, an early colonial administrator, an animal photographer and, quite recently, the local chief's sister. The monster was dispatched under suitably dramatic circumstances, and what did our traveller find in its stomach? The missionary's cross, the administrator's watch, the photographer's lens and the woman's bangles! The reader need not search the bibliography for the titles of these amusing books. I have not included them, but they were taken quite seriously by people who should have known better.

The Estuarine crocodile has a reputation at least as sinister as that of its cousin from the Nile. It is often made out to be the most voracious man-eater among crocodilians, but this assessment may be influenced by the large size this species is officially allowed to attain. There certainly have been many fatalities. Some may have been due to a marked aggressiveness at breeding time, when these crocodiles are said to attack and upset small boats crossing their path. The species, however, certainly preys on man. The saltwater crocodiles of the Sunderbans in particular have always been described as man-eating monsters of the worst kind. They have now become so rare even in that area of swampy jungles that the World Wildlife Fund Expedition led by Guy Mountfort only met three of them!

A fair amount of man-eating has been reported from Borneo, and more from New Guinea. Such a reliable witness as E. T. Gilliard, the American ornithologist, has described the saltwater crocodile as more deadly than the sharks that infest the coastal waters, and Father Dupeyrat, after a long residence on Papua Gulf, refers to it as a 'disastrous scourge'. An American entomologist, P. J. Darlington, stationed in New Guinea during World War II, was one day crouched on a partly submerged log searching for mosquito larvae, when all at once he saw a crocodile rising towards him. Trying to reach firm ground in a hurry he slipped, fell into the water and immediately had both arms grabbed by the monster. Dragging him towards the deep water, the crocodile kept rolling over and over, whirling him round, but Darlington fought back, struggling and kicking so forcefully that the reptile had to relinquish its hold.

It was this war that provided the Estuarine crocodile with what was probably the biggest man-eating orgy any crocodilians have ever been offered. During the reconquest of Burma, British troops drove over 1,000 Japanese infantrymen into the mangrove swamps between Ramree Island and the Burmese mainland. The Japanese had expected to be taken off by their ships, but they found the coast blockaded by the Royal Navy and came under heavy fire in a wilderness of mud and water, unable either to advance or to retreat. As darkness fell, the numerous crocodiles became active, and if ever hell was let loose on earth, it was in that mangrove swamp on the Bay of Bengal. The men on the British ships were horrified by the din that went on all through the night, the screams and yells of the soldiers, the thrashing of the reptiles as they rolled over, tearing their victims apart. When morning came there were twenty survivors. Some of the Japanese were certainly killed by gunfire, others drowned, but the majority seem to have been eaten by crocodiles.

The story sounds like something out of an 'Adventure Magazine', but it has been told by an American biologist, Bruce Wright, who was with the British troops and saw it all. Gruesome as the incident certainly was, it should not be allowed to influence our attitude towards crocodiles, for it resulted from a situation created entirely by human agency.

In the statistics on fatalities through wild animals published in India during the 1920s and 1930s, the victims of crocodiles were not usually specified, and this gives a good indication that losses cannot have been very high. One begins to wonder just how voracious those Sunderbans crocodiles really were.

As far as the mugger is concerned, G. P. Sanderson, in his classic *Thirteen Years among the Wild Beasts of India*, has this to say:

> The few crocodiles that are found in the Mysore rivers very rarely attack people, and fishermen—who pay no heed to them—have told me that if they come upon a crocodile whilst following their employment, it will skulk at the bottom and not move though handled, apparently believing it escapes observation. Crocodiles are like other wild creatures, very timid where not encouraged, as is sometimes done by superstitious natives. Incredible although it may seem to readers with no knowledge of the saurians but that derived from stories of their boldness elsewhere, I may instance having seen several 'bestas' (the professional boatmen, divers and fishermen of Mysore) dive time after time into water, twelve feet deep, and bring to the surface by the tail a crocodile seven feet long which I had wounded.

The Hindu custom of burning the dead on the banks of the Ganges and other rivers, the remains—often not even half consumed by the flames—afterwards being thrown into the water, gives crocodiles plenty of opportunity to feed on human flesh, and the presence of

bangles, anklets and earrings in a mugger's stomach does not neces-
sarily mean that the late wearer of these ornaments has been killed by
the reptile. A mugger—the 'Mugger of Muggerghat'—is, after all,
one of the main characters of Rudyard Kipling's delightful story
'The Undertakers'. Even though Dunbar Brander did find human
remains in the stomachs of muggers that most probably had never
been anywhere near a burning-ghat, it can nevertheless be said that
the toll taken by them has been small, in no way comparable to that
of the Nile and saltwater crocodiles, and that confirmed man-eaters
are extremely rare or non-existent.

There is no record of a gavial ever having killed a human being,
and women's ornaments which have occasionally been found in a
stomach were most certainly picked up together with a partly cremated
limb. Charles Barrett, the Australian naturalist, tells of swimming in
deep river pools among Johnston's crocodiles, and there is general
agreement that this species is harmless. The same applies to the Dwarf
crocodile and Long-nosed crocodile of West Africa.

On Biscayne Bay a man once shot an American crocodile, then
walked up to it and gave it a kick. This brought the reptile back to
life, and it attacked the hunter, mauling him so badly that he died.
This is the only fatality ever reliably recorded for this species. Kenneth
Vinton, with a long experience of Central and South America, says
that the American crocodile is a dangerous customer when cornered,
but certainly cannot be classified as a man-eater. The Orinoco crocodile,
with a muzzle almost as long and narrow as a gavial's, feeds mainly
on fish, and there seems to be absolutely no reason to regard it as in
any way harmful to man.

Of the caimans, only the jacaré-açu, the Black caiman, has definitely
been implicated, but attacks are rare and probably more or less accidental. Bates came to the conclusion that the natives of the Amazon
region both despised and feared this species. They paid little attention
to the caimans they encountered while out fishing, but some precautions were usually taken when the people went to the river bank
to wash themselves. In his many years of travelling and collecting,
Bates heard of only one well authenticated fatality: While he was
staying at Caiçara, the elderly justice of the peace of this place saw a
drunken Indian wade out into the muddy river where a big caiman
was known to lurk. He called out a warning, but the man paid no

attention, and a pair of gaping jaws suddenly appeared above the surface, seized the man round the waist and drew him under. After his experiences with the crocodiles of the Blue Nile, Rittlinger, who once paddled down the Amazon, talked of caimans as 'harmless aquarium specimens'.

Female caimans have been known to attack viciously in defence of the nest. Alligators will do the same, and a few people have been bitten, but there is no evidence of an alligator ever having killed a human being. As far as man-eating goes, the American alligator can be given a clean bill.

# 7. Veneration and Persecution

*Two Howartis harpooning a crocodile* (Baker: The Nile Tributaries of Abyssinia)

THERE have been many attempts to find a label for the time we live in: it has been called the 'Nuclear Age', the 'Age of the Common Man', and it could equally well be called the 'Age of Tourism'. There is, of course, nothing really new on earth: nuclear processes in the sun have been giving us light and warmth on our long climb from amoeba to fish and from fish to primate; the 'common man' has been around for as long as humanity has existed, forming a background to the 'uncommon man', just as he does today; and tourism, too, was with us long before Thomas Cook took it in hand. Egypt, for instance, was a tourist country 2,000 years ago, with Romans and Greeks marvelling at the pyramids, admiring the painted tombs, wandering through the colonnades of the Ramesseum, and even scratching their names on monuments.

Among these tourists of antiquity was the geographer Strabo, who lived from 63 BC to AD 20 and made full use of the 'Pax Romana' to see as much of the known world as possible. Before he departed for the Nile Valley, he is sure to have prepared himself by reading the most authoritative work on Egypt available in his time, and he must have found it very useful, even though it had been written more than 400 years earlier. It was, of course, the celebrated account of Egypt given by Herodotus, and we can imagine Strabo being very intrigued by something his great predecessor has to say regarding crocodiles:

> Some Egyptians regard the crocodile as a sacred animal, others consider it as their worst enemy. The former live around Lake Moeris, the latter near Elephantine. The former bring up a crocodile and tame it until they can handle it. They give it a life of splendour, fastening golden rings beset with jewels to its ears and golden bangles to its fore feet. They feed it with cakes and with the meat of sacrificed animals.

Lake Moeris was in Fayum, and near it stood the capital of this fertile province, Arsinoë, the city named after the sister—and wife—of Ptolemy II. Of what he saw at Arsinoë, Strabo wrote:

> A crocodile that has been tamed by the priests is kept in a lake. He is called Suchos. He is fed with the bread, meat and wine which strangers always bring when they come to see him. Our friend and host, who was one of the notabilities of the place and who took us everywhere, came to the lake with us, having saved from our luncheon a cake, a piece of the roast and a small flagon of honey. We met the crocodile on the shore of the lake. Priests

approached him and while one of them held open its jaws, another put in
the cake and the meat and poured in the honey-wine. After that the animal
dived into the lake and swam towards the opposite shore. Another visitor
arrived, also bringing his offering. The priest ran round the lake with the
food he had brought and fed it to the crocodile in the same manner.

Herodotus had known Arsinoë as Crocodilopolis, the City of
Crocodiles, and it was a very ancient place when he saw it, dating
back to the time of the Theban pharaohs of the Twelfth Dynasty.
Under the name of Shedet it was already then, about 2200 BC, a centre
of crocodile worship.

The Egyptian pantheon was remarkable for the number of deities
that were supposed to manifest themselves in the form of animals.
It cannot be said that the animals themselves were regarded as gods;
they only served as their 'theophanies' or living images, but this
association did give them divine powers and a sacred status. The gods,
on the other hand, were usually depicted with the heads of the animals
representing them on earth. Anubis, for instance, had the head of a
jackal, and Thoth, the God of Wisdom, that of an ibis. Hathor, the
Sky Goddess was cow-headed, Bastet cat-headed, and Set, once the
Lord of Upper Egypt and later the God of Evil, pig-headed. A falcon's
head characterised Horus, and the head of a lioness Sekhmet, the
terrible Goddess of Fire, War and Battle. The Water God Sebek had
the crocodile as his living incarnation, and he, therefore, wore a
crocodile's head.

Sebek, called Suchos by the Greeks, was regarded as the protector
of Fayum, and this explains the high degree of veneration he enjoyed
in Shedet, later to become Arsinoë. He also was the patron of the
pharaohs of the Thirteenth Dynasty, several of whom made use of
his name in combinations such as Sebekhetep, meaning 'Sebek is
satisfied'. Ombos in Upper Egypt, now called Kom Ombo, had a
temple dedicated to crocodile worship.

Herodotus tells us that after death the tame crocodiles were embalmed
and placed in sacred tombs. 'Such burials,' he adds, 'take place in the
subterranean chambers of the Labyrinth on Lake Moeris, close to
Crocodilopolis.'

Mummified crocodiles have been found in many rock tombs, and
those of Fayum were of very great importance to Egyptology, because
they happened to be packed in papyri. Visiting some tombs near
Thebes, Geoffroy St Hilaire noticed the perforated scales where

golden rings had been fastened. The caves of Maabdeh, opposite Manfalt, contained thousands of crocodile mummies, all of them wrapped in linen cloths soaked in bitumen. When Brehm visited the caves he could not help wondering at the sight of these stacks of mummified reptiles; they were of all sizes, from new born animals to huge monsters, the small ones piled into palm-leaf baskets sixty to eighty at a time. Eggs, too, had been deposited in these tombs. Were those really the remains of sacred crocodiles? Or were they animals that had been destroyed by hunters?

Herodotus had, after all, made it quite clear that some Egyptians regarded the crocodiles with considerable hostility. There were in actual fact several 'Theophanies', to which benevolent powers were attributed in some parts of the Nile Valley, that the inhabitants of neighbouring regions thought highly malevolent. The crocodile was one of them, the pig and the scorpion were others. Many people regarded Sebek as a god with a somewhat tarnished reputation, for after the murder of Osiris he had facilitated the escape of Set by letting him take shelter within the body of a crocodile.

As late as AD 335 sacred crocodiles were still being fed by priests at Arsinoë, but monotheistic domination of Egypt—first Christian and then Islamic—finally brought an end to this form of worship. Some religious superstitions did, however, remain attached to the saurians, and Sonnini found the following belief among Coptic monks:

> They are persuaded, that the crocodile, connoisseur enough to distinguish the Christian from the Mussulman, only attacks the latter, but respects the worshipper of Christ. They are so much prepossessed in favour of their opinion, that they bathe without fear in the waters of the Nile, where these huge and hideous lizards exist; whilst the Mahometans, whose credulity urges them to acknowledge a predilection miraculously occasioned, dare not expose themselves there. I remember to have read something similar to this in the first volume of a description of Western Ethiopia. The author affirms that the Christians have nothing to fear from crocodiles, but that they devour many negroes.

The crocodile cult of the Nile Valley probably originated very far back in pre-dynastic times, and ramifications of it have turned up all over the African continent. During his many years as a district commissioner in Ashanti, A. W. Cardinall became intimately acquainted with that land and its inhabitants. Making a thorough study of Ashanti customs, he came to realise that animals were often looked upon as members of the family, almost as 'animal brothers'. Such associations usually resulted from some ancient tradition, handed down from generation to generation, according to which the animal in question had once befriended an ancestor of the family. The crocodile, strangely enough, was most often thought to have played such a part, and Cardinall found it protected for past services among the Dagomba, Konkomba, Kassena, Manfussi and Dagabi. Of all the animal cults practised in Ashanti, that of the crocodile was by far the most common. The reptiles were perhaps not exactly worshipped, but great respect was paid to them.

In the neighbouring Ivory Coast the crocodile is closely associated with Queen Abra Poku, the founder of the Kingdom of Baule, and even today the reptiles can often be seen represented in wood or metal, usually with some prey held in the mouth. In former times, when the Akan people from what is now Ghana crossed the Comoe River into the Baule country, they never failed to offer sacrifices to the crocodiles.

Strabo's account of 'Suchos', the Arsinoë crocodile, being called out and fed brings to mind 'Lutembe', and we can only regret that we have absolutely no indication of how this animal came to be associated with the fishermen of Murchison Gulf. 'Lutembe' is, however, not the only tame crocodile that has been seen or heard of in tropical Africa. Boyd Alexander, the English explorer and ornithologist, found a pond with sacred crocodiles near the Nigerian village of Wukari. The people were obviously on the best of terms with the reptiles, and all day long women could be seen moving around among the saurians, washing clothes and drawing water. While searching for the almost legendary pygmy hippopotamus in the forests of Liberia, Hans Schomburgk photographed a sacred crocodile in the village of Sugary. It left the water at the witch doctor's call and was rewarded with a chicken. The villagers venerated it as their protective deity, but they did not stand for any nonsense from their scaly god: when the crocodile had the temerity to grab a calf, the witch doctor called it out and gave it a thorough hiding. This may be quite a good way to deal with a living god !

In the course of his important journeys of exploration, Henry M. Stanley recorded many strange customs and came across many a wonderful tale. On Ukerewe Island in Lake Victoria he was told that the chief of neighbouring Ukara Island had great power over crocodiles. One of these reptiles was said to live in his house and to be as docile and obedient as a dog and as intelligent as a human being. It fed from the chief's hand and carried out any order it was given. When the chief of Ukara coveted one of the inmates of the chief of Ukerewe's harem, he communicated this desire to the crocodile and bade it lie in wait among the rushes where the woman used to bathe. It was then to seize and convey her without injury across the 8 mile channel to Ukara. The very next day the woman was in the house of the chief of Ukara.

When Stanley expressed certain doubts as to the veracity of this story, his informant became most indignant and assured him that the father of the present chief of Ukerewe had owned a crocodile, too, and that this animal once stole the wife of an Arab and carried her across the country to its master's home. Stanley had no opportunity to ascertain whether there might be some foundation to all this talk, but Father Huard, a missionary who resided on Ukerewe long after his visit, made some discoveries that fitted in well with what the explorer had been told. He found that crocodiles, though not regarded as gods or spirits, were highly respected by the islanders. The 'balogi' or witch-doctors were generally credited with being able to arrange for the transmigration of a dead person's soul into one of these saurians, which was then thought to become almost a part of the sorcerer. If he ordered it to go and get a certain person, the animal would do this quickly and efficiently. So whenever somebody was caught by a crocodile, the Wakerewe began an immediate search for the 'mulogi' who had sent the man-eater, and some innocent wretch was sure to be smelt out and executed.

Crocodiles as familiars or 'alter egos' of sorcerers were by no means restricted to Ukerewe Island. The Rev W. Holman Bentley, one of the pioneer missionaries on the Congo and a very reliable observer of man and nature, wrote in 1900:

> In districts where crocodiles are common, the witches are believed some-times to turn into crocodiles or to enter and actuate them, and so to cause their victim's death by catching him. Where leopards are common, the witches may become leopards. The natives often positively affirm that a crocodile, of itself, is a harmless creature. So thoroughly do they believe this, that in some places they go into the river to catch whitebait, or to attend to their fish traps without hesitation. If one of them is eaten by a crocodile they hold their witch palavers, find and kill the witch and go on as before.
>
> At Lukunga, one of the stations of the American Baptist Mission, a great

crocodile came out of the Lukunga River to attack the pigsty in the night. The pig smelt the reptile and began to make such a noise that Mr. Ingham, the missionary got up. When he found the cause, he shot the crocodile. In the morning he skinned it, and found in the stomach the anklets of two women. They were at once recognized as belonging to women who had disappeared at different times, when fetching water. I was at the station a few days later, and one of my Congo workmen, who was with me, warmly denied that the crocodile ate the women. He maintained that they never did so. But what about the anklets? Were they not proof positive that, in this case, the crocodile had eaten the women? No, he caught the women and handed them over to the witch who worked through him; as for the anklets, it must have been his fashion to take them as perquisites.

Among the Konde inhabiting the lands at the northern end of Lake Nyasa, bewitching a crocodile to kill an enemy used to be considered an especially heinous crime, and the punishment was appropriate: the person considered as the offender was put into a fish trap and left in the water until a crocodile came and ate him. A crocodile was mentioned as the familiar of a witch in a fairly recent Rhodesian court case.

Most people have heard of 'Leopard Men' and 'Lion Men', but it is much less generally known that associations of 'Crocodile Men' existed not so very long ago in Sierra Leone, in the Ivory Coast and on the banks of the Congo. Crocodile masks, stuffed skins and canoes shaped like crocodiles figured prominently in their ceremonials, and there have been a number of court cases concerning murders committed by initiates. Various reasons have been given for these killings. One authority on African secret societies gives it as his opinion that they were committed in order to obtain possession of certain organs of the victims, such as the heart, the lungs and the brain, which were then eaten for magical purposes.

The big island of Madagascar has no large terrestrial carnivores—no lions, leopards, wild dogs or hyenas—nor are there any really venomous snakes. This leaves the crocodile as the only animal dangerous to man, and it has, therefore, become the focus of the cults and superstitions which in all parts of the world have been directed towards the dominant predator of the area—the bear in northern countries, the wolf in Central Europe, the jaguar in Mexico, the tiger in various parts of southern Asia, and the lion and leopard on the African continent, with the hyena and the crocodile as close seconds.

In his interesting book on the fauna of Madagascar, Raymond

Decary gives a good summary of the highly important part the crocodile has played in Malagasy beliefs and customs. He mentions a number of places where there are, or were, sacred crocodiles, one of the most famous being Lake Anivorano in Antakarana, the northernmost part of the island, and only 75 kilometres from Diego Suarez. According to a local legend there used to be a big and prosperous village on the present site of Lake Anivorano, and its inhabitants were not exactly renowned for their hospitality. When a wandering stranger one day asked for a drink of water, he received gruff refusals all round, and only one old woman treated him with kindness. The stranger happened to be a great sorcerer, and after having ordered the old woman to gather her family and to leave forthwith, he put a curse on the village and caused it to be swallowed up by the waters rising out of the earth. This, incidentally, is a story with a wide distribution. It turns up, with certain variations, in many parts of Europe, and Verney Lovett Cameron came across it at Lake Dilolo in Angola. But while the people living round Lake Dilolo will tell you that in the stillness of the night you can hear the pounding of corn, the singing of women, the crowing of cocks and the bleating of goats, the villagers who disappeared in Lake Anivorano were all changed into crocodiles.

The inhabitants of a place not far from the lake consider themselves to be the descendants of the woman who escaped the catastrophe, and for a long time they have been holding celebrations on the lake shore, with much singing and dancing, and with the slaughter of oxen to feed the crocodiles. As Decary describes it, big lumps of meat were deposited close to the water, and the saurians came up to grab them without paying the least attention to the crowds and to the festive commotion. David Attenborough went to film this ceremony a few years ago, but he found that it had degenerated into a show put on for the benefit of tourists.

In former times the entrails of the dead Sakalava kings were fed to the crocodiles of Lake Komakoma, which naturally became imbued with a very special kind of sanctity. The crocodiles of the Kindroma also enjoyed very strict protection, for this river flows past the tombs of the Maroseranana Dynasty, and whenever oxen were offered up to the 'manes' of the rulers, the saurians got their full share of the sacrifice.

Wherever there were sacred crocodiles it was considered as 'fady'—

taboo—to brandish a spear over the water. In some places there was a prohibition on throwing grass or mud into the water, as this was thought to insult the reptiles.

In the country of the Antandroy a woman was once caught in a fish trap, together with a 'voay'—a crocodile—which she had married. She gave birth to two sons and then returned to the river and to her reptilian husband. The sons became the ancestors of the clan of the Zafandravoay—the Sons of the Crocodile—whose members will never kill one of the reptiles and are persuaded that they can traverse the most dangerous river without coming to any harm. When a Zafandravoay dies, a nail is hammered through his forehead to prevent him from moving. This is taken out again after the body has been placed into the family tomb and at the same time the corpse is told to join the ancestors in the water. It is thought to change into a crocodile immediately after the tomb has been closed and to go off to the river. An ox is sacrificed to it each year. Among the Antandroy almost everybody has a crocodile as a 'protector'.

In the southern and south-western parts of the island certain individuals known as 'tomponboay', are able to call the 'voay' out of the water. One branch of the Antanosy tribe had a tame crocodile—something like a Malagasy 'Lutembe'—which was regarded as the reincarnation of a dead child. It came to the call of the child's father, who happened to be a 'tomponboay'.

Among the Antarkare, the Sakalava, and the northern Betsimisaraka, there was formerly a general belief that the souls of dead chiefs entered the bodies of crocodiles. Chapelier, a French naturalist, who visited Madagascar over 150 years ago, knew of a chief in the Bay of Antongil who regarded a huge crocodile inhabiting a nearby pool as his ancestor. Every year he offered it a young man and a girl as a sacrifice, the victims, bedecked with jewellery, being suspended over the pool in a forked pole until great-grandfather condescended to claim them.

While it is difficult to decide just how common or uncommon human sacrifices of this kind were in old-time Madagascar, there is no doubt about the widespread acceptance, especially in the southern regions, of the 'ordeal by crocodile'. The 'voay' were generally credited with being able to distinguish right from wrong, just from unjust, and never to attack a person with a perfectly clear conscience. According to the Sieur Dubois, who spent four years in Madagascar at the end of the eighteenth-century, people frequently submitted to the ordeal of their own free will. In the midst of a heated legal debate a man would exclaim, 'May the "voay" eat me, if I have done what I am accused of,' and he would then proceed to traverse the nearest river.

De Lacombe was present in 1840 when a young woman accused of having had an affair with a slave found herself condemned to undergo the ordeal. During the night of the full moon she entered the river, submerged herself three times close to an island that was a favourite haunt of the saurians, and then safely reached the opposite bank. The accuser was ordered to pay her a heavy indemnity. Some authors think that such ordeals were secretely performed until fairly recent times.

James Sibree, the English missionary-naturalist, found the people inhabiting the shores of Lake Itasy convinced that the 'voay' exacted a human life for every one of their kind killed by hunters. When three French travellers shot a crocodile, there was an uproar all round the lake, the locals being apprehensive of undeserved reptilian retribution, and the Europeans had to leave in a hurry in order to save their lives.

Hindus regard the big reptiles as being dedicated to Vishnu, the creator and ruler of the water, and crocodile worship of one kind or another has, therefore, been reported from all over India. It most often manifested itself in village tanks having their resident mugger, which could be seen basking in the sun, with women bathing and cleaning their bronze pots not twenty paces away. Some of these sacred muggers may even have been brought to the tanks by the villagers themselves.

The great crocodilian showpiece of the Indian subcontinent has always been the 'mugger-peer'—the crocodile pond of Karachi. It is now in Pakistan, of course, but it was India when Andrew Leith Adams saw it in the 1860s. The description he gave of the 'mugger-peer' sounds very much like an echo of what Strabo wrote after his visit to Arsinoë:

> The great pond is about 300 yards in circumference and contains many little grassy islands, on which the majority of the crocodiles was then basking; some were asleep on its slimy sides, others half submerged in the muddy water, while now and then a huge monster would raise himself upon its diminutive legs, and waddling for a few paces, fall flat on his belly. Young ones from a foot in length and upwards, ran nimbly along the margin of the

pond, disappearing suddenly in the turbid waters as soon as we approached. The largest crocodile lives in a long, narrow tank separated from the others. The Fakirs and natives who worship in the neighbouring temples, have painted his forehead red—they venerate the old monster, making a salaam to his majesty whenever he shows himself above water. A handsome young Baloochee, whose occupation it was to feed the animals, informed us that the said kind was upwards of two hundred years old! (?) and that by way of a 'tit-bit' he was in the habit of devouring the young crocodiles.

Strangers are expected to stand treat, not only by the Fakirs and natives, who gain a livelihood by hanging about the pond, and showing the monsters, but even the crocodiles themselves seem to anticipate a feast, and on the arrival of a party come out in unusual numbers. Accordingly we had a goat slaughtered, during which operation the brutes seemed to rouse themselves, as if preparing for a rush. Then one guide, taking piece after piece of flesh, dashed it on the bank, uttering a low, gurgling sound, at which the whole tank became in motion, and crocodiles of whose existence we had been before ignorant, splashed through the shallow water, struggling which should seize the prize. The shore was literally covered with scaly monsters, snapping their jaws at one another.

The saurians play an important part in the spiritual world of the Papuans. The Kiwai, for instance, have a very involved creation myth from which the crocodile emerges as their father. Among the tribes of the Sepik River, so famous for their artistic achievements, most persons identify themselves with animals—with parrots, hornbills, turtles and especially with crocodiles, which are admired for their strength and cunning and for their mastery of the water. The various totem animals are used extensively in decorative art, and representations of crocodiles, therefore, appear frequently on bowls, drums and other utensils. The Sepik people like to carve the prows of their canoes in the shape of a crocodile's head, which is usually very lifelike in its expression though somewhat stylised in execution. According to Behrmann, one of the early explorers of the Sepik, these heads are often combined with human faces or with birds. Dancing masks in the form of crocodiles' heads are widely distributed.

Dahl's guide on the Daly River of Arnhem Land, an aborigine who went under the name of 'Buckley', insisted that he had fathers, brothers and uncles among the crocodiles. When the Norwegian naturalist shot a specially big specimen, Buckley said sorrowfully that now the 'old man', the chief of the crocodiles, had been killed and that its ghost would certainly haunt the party. The mosquitoes became very troublesome soon afterwards, and the aborigine lamented:

The spirits of the crocodiles are offended, you see. You have shot small crocodiles. Holm has shot a grown up crocodile. No matter. But you have shot the old man crocodile, my brother, and he now takes revenge. He has told the mosquitoes that five men are sitting in Buckley's camp who all the time shoot the old men among the crocodiles.

Wherever they occur, crocodiles have become part of the local folklore, and it is interesting to find that in Asian and African fables they do not so much play the part of fierce all-devouring dragons but rather that of simpletons who are duped by other animals. Here, for instance, are two tales from Celebes:

One fine day a monkey was swimming in a river, when a crocodile caught him by the leg. 'Oh, you haven't got hold of my leg', the monkey said and added: 'This is my leg,' at the same time showing the attacker a piece of wood. The crocodile loosened his hold, seized the stick and let the monkey escape.

Another monkey was stranded on a little island in a river, and a crocodile came and said he would eat him up. 'Very well', answered the monkey, 'but you are too small. Go and fetch some companions first, and then you can feast on me.' The crocodile went away and soon came back with a number of friends. 'Now,' said the monkey, 'stand in a row side by side that I may count to see if there are enough of you.' The crocodiles did this, and the monkey jumped on the back of the nearest, and then on to the next, counting as he went, until he came to the end of the row. From the back of the last crocodile he jumped on to the river bank and escaped.

In a Laotian fable it is the gibbon, described as still having a long tail, which plays all sorts of tricks on the crocodile. The saurian eventually becomes infuriated and bites off the ape's tail—since that day the gibbons are tailless—but feels so disgusted at having been made to lose face that it throws itself down the cataract of the river.

In African folk tales Sungura, the hare, usually makes a fool of everybody else. On one occasion Sungura saw the elephant standing among the trees and went up to it with a rope. 'Elephant, I am much stronger than you,' Sungura said. 'If you don't believe it, take that rope and we shall have a tug-of-war.' The elephant shook with laughter at the idea of being challenged by Sungura, but he nevertheless grabbed the rope. Holding on to the other end, Sungura ran to the river and called out: 'Crocodile, I am much stronger than you. If you don't believe it, take that rope and we shall have a tug-of-war'. The crocodile accepted the challenge, thinking: 'I shall soon have silly little Sungura in the water, and then I will make a meal of him'. Sungura now hid behind a tree and called out: 'Pull!' The elephant and the crocodile pulled and struggled till they dropped with fatigue, but by that time Sungura had quietly stolen away.

The ancient Egyptians had many legends concerning crocodiles. They believed them to have no tongue, which may be excusable, since this organ is fixed to the lower palate for its whole length. It does seem strange, though, that they also regarded them as completely voiceless; one would think that they would occasionally have heard the bellowing mating calls, but the crocodile was for them the personification of silence, and this may well have led to its association with the god Sebek.

The ichneumon was not only credited with eating crocodiles' eggs—which it most certainly does—but also with destroying the crocodiles themselves. Pliny gave the following account of how the mongoose was supposed to achieve this feat:

> Now when he [the crocodile] is lulled as it were, fast asleep with his pleasure and contentment the rat of India, or Ichneumon, spies his vantage and seeing him lie thus broad gaping, whips into his mouth and shoots himself down his throat as quick as an arrow and then gnaws his bowels, eating a hole through his belly.

The story found full credence in Europe and remained for a long time an accepted part of crocodile-lore.

Europeans were equally fascinated by the well known legend to which we owe the expression 'Crocodile's tears'. It is not quite clear where the term originated, and some authors think that it did not come from the East but emanated from France, probably from some monks indulging in flights of allegoric and symbolic fancies. The legend was known to Bartholomaeus Anglicus, a Franciscan who taught in Paris around 1225. In his encyclopaedia of the natural sciences—or what went under that name in his time—he quoted it in the following words: 'If the crocodile findeth a man by the brim of the water, or by the cliff, he slayeth him if he may, and then he weepeth upon him and swalloweth him at last'.

This was, of course, a bit of unnatural history no self-respecting author could pass by. In *Mandeville's Travels*—written at Liège in 1357 by an unknown author who most probably never left Europe—it was included among a crop of eastern marvels which were lapped up avidly by a gullible public. We may laugh at the tremendous impact this work of fictional travels had in its time, but, in view of the success recently achieved by a book dealing with equally fictional spatial invasions of the primeval earth, one comes to the sad conclusion that the general public is hardly less credulous in our days. The crocodile shedding its hypocritical tears certainly became well established through *Mandeville's Travels*. Shakespeare made use of it, and the story was still widely believed at the beginning of the eighteenth-century, so that Johan Jakob Scheuchzer, a town physician of Zurich like Gesner and an excellent naturalist, found himself compelled to write: 'The foundations and substance of this famous old tale are so feeble that today we would be well advised to do without it.'

In his famous 'Historie of Foure-footed Beastes', which was published in London in 1607, Edward Topsell preserved another intriguing bit of fable when he wrote that according to some people you could chase away a crocodile by closing the left eye and staring at it fixedly with the right.

We have seen that the veneration of crocodiles in ancient Egypt was by no means universal. In some places the reptiles were regarded as associates of the sinister Set, and thus as creatures to be hated by every true worshipper of the Sun God Horus. Sacred to the inhabitants of Ombos, they were persecuted with implacable enmity by the people of Tentyra, and bitter quarrels sometimes broke out between the two towns. The Tentyrites gained considerable fame as crocodile hunters, and some of them were brought to Rome in order to perform in the Circus Flaminius. Pliny tells us that a Tentyrite would pursue a crocodile into the water, overtake it, spring on its back and force a stick into its mouth by which, as with a bit, he guided it to the shore where it was put to death. One wonders whether this might not be another one of the tall stories which so invariably crop up when there is talk of crocodiles. The Tentyrites may well have performed this trick in the pool of the Circus Flaminius for the edification of Roman crowds—but how did they tackle the saurians back home in the River Nile?

Considering the high reputation for daring the Tentyrites managed to acquire, it seems strange that no contemporary pictorial representations of their exploits have ever come to light. While the harpooning of hippos has been portrayed dramatically by Egyptian artists, there are very few representations of crocodile hunting. One forms part of a sculptured relief in the temple of Edfu and shows the wicked Set in the guise of a crocodile being attacked by Horus wielding a harpoon. This shows that crocodiles were harpooned in ancient Egypt, as they were in the Sudan until quite recently, and the illustration in Baker's *Nile Tributaries of Abyssinia* of two howartis—hippo hunters—stalking a crocodile on the Setit River could well give us a good idea of how the reptiles were hunted by the Tentyrites when they did not have to show off in Rome.

Baker gives the following description of the hunt:

> The howartis, having studied the wind, ascended for about a quarter of a mile, and then swam across the river, harpoon in hand. The two men reached the opposite bank, beneath which they alternately waded or swam down the stream towards the spot upon which the crocodile was lying. Thus advancing under cover of the steep bank or floating with the stream in deep places and crawling like crocodiles across the shallows, the two hunters at length arrived at the bank of rushes on the other side of which the monster was basking asleep upon the sand. They were now about waistdeep and they kept close to the rushes with their harpoons raised, ready to cast the moment they should pass the rush bed and come in view of the crocodile. Thus steadily advancing, they had just arrived at the corner within about eight yards of the crocodile, when the creature either saw them or obtained their wind; in an instant it rushed to the water, at the same moment the two harpoons were launched with great rapidity by the hunters. One glanced obliquely from the scales, the other stuck fair in the tough hide and the iron detached from the bamboo, held fast, while the ambatch float, sunning on the surface of the water, marked the course of the reptile.

Tentyrites may perhaps also have had a way of spearing crocodiles from boats. Some Hausa who had wandered across Africa to the marshes of the Sudan made a living that way not so many years ago, going out at night and using electric lights. The Egyptians could have spotted the shiny crocodiles' eyes by the light of torches.

In India, as in ancient Egypt, veneration and persecution went side by side. While villagers implored passing sportsmen not to shoot the sacred mugger in the nearby tank, fishermen, having spotted a mugger in a shallow pool, surrounded the submerged reptile with nets and then immobilised it completely by sticking two bamboo poles into the mud on each side of the neck. A rope was next passed round the helpless animal, the poles were removed and the nets drawn over it. As soon as the mugger had become properly entangled, it was hauled out of the water. The fishermen of the Indus had a method of netting gavials on their basking grounds.

Some of the Malagasy tribes and clans claiming descent from

crocodiles nevertheless drew a line at being eaten by their brothers. Whenever somebody was taken, the local chief went to the lake or river and pronounced a solemn accusation. A crocodile was then caught on a baited hook, and after it had been pulled out of the water, the chief approached the animal, apologising profusely for having to treat a dear relative in this way. Spears being 'fady', the captured reptile had to be killed with fire-hardened poles. As soon as it was dead, the women let down their hair as a sign of mourning, uttered howls and lamentations and enveloped the carcase with silken cords, symbolising a shroud, before it was ceremoniously buried like a human corpse.

Primitive peoples in various parts of the world have come up with ingenious devices for catching crocodilians. The contraption used by the Indians of the Essequibo River in British Guyana was made famous by that somewhat eccentric naturalist, Charles Waterton. It consisted of four sharp unbarbed prongs tied to the end of a rope, with pegs forced between the prongs so that their upper ends diverged. An acouchy, a rabbit-sized rodent, was used as bait, its intestines wound tightly round the elastic prongs so as to compress and hold them close to the rope. They could thus easily pass down a caiman's throat, only to expand again within its stomach.

Having got this 'hook' ready, Waterton's Indian hunter fixed it to the end of a 2 ft pole, which was rammed obliquely into the river bank so that the bait dangled a foot from the water, the end of the rope being tied to a stake firmly driven into the sand. The Indian then beat an empty tortoise shell with an axe. He told Waterton that this was to let the caimans know that something was going on. A caiman did in fact swallow the bait, and as it was being hauled in, flamboyant Waterton vaulted on to its back and came riding out of the river, seated on the saurian like Arion on the dolphin.

The 'alir', which was much in use in Malaya and Sarawak, would probably have delighted Heath Robinson. Its main part was a stick of hardwood, 10 in long and 1 in in diameter, somewhat crescentic in shape and sharply pointed at both ends. One end of a 6 ft line made of tough strips of green bark, which could not be chewed through in a hurry, was fastened to a long rattan rope and the other end was fastened to the two-pointed piece of wood. One half of the stick was then loosely tied to the bark rope with a piece of string that could easily be broken by a sharp pull. When the 'alir', baited with a fish, finally hung 6 in above the water, the stick, held parallel to the rope, could be swallowed without difficulty. It was hoped that a pull on the rope would then break the string and draw it crosswise in the crocodile's stomach.

On the lower Congo crocodiles were caught with a similar 'hook', which consisted of two crossed pieces of wood.

The South American Indians used to catch caimans for their flesh, which they considered a great delicacy. Having killed one, they would immediately roast the tail and the head, cut up the body and boil the intestines. Apart from the bones and the skin, no part of the carcase was wasted.

The Estuarine crocodiles which Dahl collected as museum specimens in Arnhem Land were eaten by the aborigines with 'all the energy produced by ravenous savage stomachs'. Crocodile meat is also much in favour in many parts of Africa, being eaten with relish by the Shilluk of the Sudan, and by the people of Sierra Leone, who consider the gall bladder to be highly poisonous and cut it out the moment the animal has been killed. There is no ban placed on eating crocodile by the laws of Islam, but African clans who have the crocodile as a totem will not touch it.

The Chinese eat the alligators of the Yangtse Valley, and crocodile meat used to be on sale in the markets of Cochin China (South Vietnam), especially in Mytho and Chodoe. Guy Cheminaud reports seeing a live specimen displayed all trussed up on a stall, its tail being sold in slices. The repeated cuts brought practically no reaction from the reptile, but one may perhaps be permitted to question who, in that case, played the part of the vile voracious brute! In old-time Siam young crocodiles were caught and brought up in special basins because the king had to eat crocodile meat on certain ceremonial occasions. It is also said to have been eaten very frequently by the Horus-worshipping inhabitants of the ancient Egyptian town of Behdet or Apollinopolis.

The meat has been described to me quite enthusiastically as resembling lobster, but I find that opinions differ. It found no favour at all with Cheminaud's French palate because of its musky flavour, despite the fact that he had a 'chef' who was able to make almost all the spoils of the chase eatable in one way or another. Dahl writes of the flesh of the saltwater crocodile: 'It would not have been bad if nothing better had been offered—it would have been pleasant had not an unsavoury smell of musk been attached to it'. Brehm found old specimens quite disgustingly musky, but this did not apply to young crocodiles, whose flesh he considered quite eatable.

Owen describes crocodiles' meat as insipid—half-meat, half-fish, something in between tough chicken and even tougher cod, neither to be recoiled from in horror nor to be given exaggerated praise. He goes on to say:

> Europeans, apt to be affected by imagination and 'the very idea', will shy off it if they know its identity, but if you camouflage it as curry and apologize for the cook having picked a bad hunk of meat in the market, they will usually eat it voraciously and politely say: 'O not at all, not at all, excellent, excellent' and give an uncertain brave smile when you later confess its true identity.

Sir John Graham Kerr's opinion of caiman flesh was: 'Excellent, like good white fish, though with a harder consistency'.

Alligator feet are said to have been served successfully in big European hotels, but there is a suspicion that the accompaniments really were the most attractive part of the dish.

When Brehm travelled in the Sudan, the musk glands fetched a price of 4 to 6 dollars, a sum for which one could then buy two heifers. They were used for compounding pomades and ointments very much in demand with the village belles of Nubia. Arab women on the Setit River sometimes wore them like beads strung on a necklace.

These glands were put to a similar use in South America, not only by the Indians but also by some of the whites residing in the interior. As they were taken out of the dead animal, the ducts had to be closed immediately by means of a tight ligature in order to prevent the loss of any liquid. They were then hung up in the shade to dry exteriorly, while the contents turned into a highly odoriferous oil of such fine consistency that it would ooze through almost any material. This oil, in very small quantities, formed the basis of various indigenous perfumes. Indians sometimes smeared themselves with it to keep the mosquitoes away, a procedure which, for the time being, turned them into exceedingly disagreeable neighbours.

A paste made of the fats of crocodiles, snakes, gazelles and hippo received high praise as an excellent hair-restorer in ancient Egypt, and it quite possibly was just as effective as most of the hair-restorers advertised today. Crocodiles' blood was thought to be a certain cure for snakebite, while ashes from a burnt skin were applied to wounds. Fat was effective against fever, toothache and mosquito bites.

Various parts of the Chinese alligator are used for medical purposes, as charms and—how could it be otherwise in view of the Chinese preoccupation with the subject—as aphrodisiacs!

While hunting in the Matebele country at the time of King Lo Bengula, Selous refrained from shooting crocodiles because he knew that anybody in possession of a crocodile's liver was thought to be able to bewitch other persons, and he did not want to have the slightest suspicion of occult practices attached to any of his men. The Wanyamwezi of East Africa also regarded the crocodile as a magical beast, with blood so venomous that it could poison whole rivers. When the explorer Boehm passed through their country he found that the Mtami, the king, for fear of being poisoned, had strictly prohibited the killing of the saurians.

In certain parts of Madagascar, crocodiles' teeth were used for decorating reliquaries containing parts of defunct kings. As the teeth had to come from a living animal, a crocodile was trapped and then trussed up in such a way that three of its teeth could be extracted. Silver rings were then fastened to its legs and it was restored to liberty as a 'razan panjaka', a royal ancestor of very special sanctity.

For thousands of years crocodiles have thus been harpooned, speared, or trapped, but this did not affect their numbers in any way. The introduction of firearms brought a change for the worse, and we have seen how the saurians gradually disappeared from most parts of Egypt. During the last century, commerce, missionary enterprise and colonial expansion brought a great influx of Europeans who usually seemed to hate the saurians with much greater intensity than the natives who had had to live with them for so long. Wherever white men travelled on a tropical river, be it on the Amazon, the Congo, the Nile, the Indus, or the Sepik, they never failed to salute practically every crocodilian with a bullet. 'I avow, with what regrets may be necessary, an active hatred of these brutes and a desire to kill them'— thus wrote Winston Churchill when he saw the crocodiles of the Victoria Nile in his *My African Journey*!

This attitude of utter abhorrence is well exemplified by the words

J. A. Hunter, one of East Africa's best known white hunters, put at the head of a chapter on crocodiles in one of his books: 'It is strange there should be a common enemy to both man and beast, but it is so, in that hideous monster, the crocodile. It can be aptly described as a loathsome beast, unloved and feared by all'. 'Hideous', 'loathsome', 'repulsive', these adjectives have been used so often that one feels they must eventually have begun to appear quite automatically whenever a writer found himself mentioning crocodiles.

Even this 'hate-the-crocodile' campaign did not seriously endanger the crocodilians. The constant bombardment from sporting rifles, the control schemes and the bounties paid by various governments for crocodiles and crocodiles' eggs thinned them out locally, but in many areas they remained as numerous as ever. A real threat to their survival only developed when they became the objects of large-scale exploitation for financial gain; that is, when Fashion turned its attention to them.

This monster exerts absolute domination over millions of women— as well as men!—and has them dancing to its tune like inanimate puppets. There might be something very amusing in this utter subjection of so many representatives of the species that proudly calls itself 'sapiens', if it were not that Fashion takes it into its head at frequent intervals to decree the ruthless exploitation of some unfortunate member of the animal kingdom. In the course of time, it has had its henchmen kill off the fur-bearers of the northern forests, devastate the seal rookeries of oceanic islands, massacre egrets and birds of paradise, murder hundreds of thousands of koala bears, club to death seal pups on the ice off the coast of Canada, trap tens of thousands of those beautiful spotted cats—leopards, snow leopards, jaguars and ocelots—and all this just to amuse the puppets and keep them within its grasp.

Fashion had had an eye on the crocodilians for a long time. As its first victim it chose the American alligator, the eradication of which it began in the last century and then greatly speeded up during the 1920s and 1930s, but it was not until the end of the 1940s and the early 1950s that it decided really to give the saurians the coup de grâce. Armies of henchmen invaded every tropical river, lake and marsh where crocodiles could be found, butchering them with deadly efficiency. At first they shot them by day on their basking grounds.

*Alligator*

Later, when the saurians had become even more shy and wary than usual, the killers changed over to night hunting, cruising round in dinghies with outboard motors and armed with strong spotlights that made the eyes of the swimming reptiles glow like jewels. They made excellent targets, but there was no need for expert marksmanship since the shooting was done at point-blank range. Sometimes the animals could literally be touched with the muzzle! It was sheer slaughter, and more crocodiles were often killed in the course of a night than the native helpers could skin.

Some skin-hunters experimented with cage traps. Wire snares and vicious W-shaped iron hooks were also used, especially by the poachers, who enthusiastically joined this lucrative enterprise.

Fashion seemed to have backed an absolute winner this time. On former occasions there had been tedious interference from people it could not control. They had fought it tooth and nail to save the egrets and birds of paradise, the seals and the koalas. They were even going into battle for the spotted cats—but who would fight for the crocodiles? Everybody hated them, and Fashion's henchmen stood a good chance of being acclaimed as popular heroes.

A fairy tale? Certainly not! It has been evident for a long time that the fashion industry lives by manipulating the masses and those who claim to defy 'manipulation' are, in fact, the most obedient of dancers. Humanity has always been manipulated—by witchdoctors, shamans, priests, kings, politicians, salesmen, confidence tricksters—and it always will be. The fashion magnates are very welcome to what they can get by uttering ponderous pronouncements on the ups and downs of skirts, but it is high time they kept their hands off wild animals— once and for all!

Meanwhile the slaughter of crocodiles for 'fashionable' handbags, shoes and other articles is still going on! With good skins valued at £1.50 per belly inch, a 9 ft specimen brings in about £40, and the killers are encouraged to comb even the remotest creeks, tributaries and marshes. This high price also induces large-scale poaching in areas where crocodiles are protected by law.

# 8. A Plea for the Crocodilians

*American crocodile* (Brehm: Tierleben)

WHAT we know of the evolutionary history of crocodilians, of their distribution and of their way of life, makes them appear an eminently successful group of animals. Having established themselves as the dominant predators of a fairly stable habitat, they held this position over a very long period, never relinquishing it to another reptile, nor to any mammal or fish. They are fecund animals, laying so many eggs that the very heavy losses suffered by the early stages have no adverse effect upon their numbers. As they live for a very long time and have few natural enemies able to harm them after they have reached maturity, these losses, due in part to their own cannibalistic tendencies, must even be regarded as very necessary, for a survival of a much higher percentage of hatchlings could lead to fatal over-crowding of the habitat. Population dynamics are thus well balanced.

Crocodilians are by no means the constant and voracious feeders they were supposed to be, and with the rivers teeming with fish, snails and other animals, there normally is no shortage of prey. In marginal areas, where they have to cope with seasonal difficulties, they have proved to be very adaptable, going into aestivation or hibernation when necessary. Surviving triumphantly when the great majority of reptiles became extinct, they were in no way affected by the mammalian domination of the Tertiary Age. The Ice Ages of the northern hemisphere restricted their area of distribution, but they held out all over the tropics and in some subtropical regions as well. Yes, the crocodilians have been quite amazingly successful, and there was only one contingency they could not cope with: the greed of modern man!

Since life first appeared on earth, innumerable species of animals have been shaped by the forces of evolution, only to vanish again after having held the stage for a longer or shorter period. They mostly succumbed to competition from closely allied species that had acquired a slight advantage in the struggle for survival. Whole groups of animals must, however, have been exterminated by much more highly developed species that invaded their homelands after having traversed newly formed land bridges. Others became the victims of climatic changes which created desert belts or brought about periods of glaciation, and we must also consider the possibility of 'phylogenetic senescence'—an ageing process that may have terminated the existence of whole families and genera. Extinction is thus nothing new, but it used to be a very gradual process extending over thousands and even hundreds of thousands of years. It has become very rapid and woefully frequent since man made himself lord and master of the earth.

Man has proved his mastery by eradicating at least fifty species of mammals and forty-nine species of birds within the last few hundred years, not to mention a very much larger number of subspecies. The number of animals that have been brought close to extinction through human agency is horrifyingly high.

It must be admitted that extermination quite often came about without man even noticing what was going on—mainly through the intentional or accidental transplantation of predatory animals and through widespread habitat destruction. Many species have, however, become extinct or been reduced to pitifully small remnants through uncontrolled exploitation. Overkilling wiped out Steller's sea cow, the great auk, the bluebuck, and the quagga, just as it endangered the bison, the sea otter, the chinchilla and the whales. Now it is the turn of the crocodilians.

Until recently the saurians showed an astonishing resistance to human persecution. They weathered the 'hate-the-croc' campaign without suffering too much damage, the thinning out of adults quite possibly easing the pressure on the youngsters and giving them a somewhat higher expectancy of survival. The holocaust of the last twenty-five years, however, was too much even for these tough and well adapted reptiles.

One hunter operating in the Lake Rukwa region is said to have had a hand in killing 45,000 crocodiles. This was the work of one man in quite a restricted area—what must be the figure of crocodilians massacred by thousands of shooters all over the tropics! This, of course, is the kind of pressure no species or group of species can endure for any length of time—but human exploiters out for quick profits seem to be quite incapable of understanding this fact! The incredibly shortsighted way in which the worldwide slaughter of crocodilians was carried out is well shown in the answer Hugh Cott received when he remonstrated with one of the shooters: 'When we finish them here', the man said, 'we go to another place'. It has always been like that—

with beavers, bison, fur seals, sea otters, whales—the exploiters moving from one place to the next until there suddenly was no place left to go.

The crocodilians have been in existence for something like 140 million years—human greed has brought most of them close to extinction in a little over two decades.

The Nile crocodile has become very scarce in many areas where it used to be common up to the end of World War II. In the course of a scientific expedition to Angola in 1953, W. Hellmich, the German herpetologist, could not find a single crocodile in the Cuanza River, where according to reliable sources they had been numerous a short time before. In the Cubal River he only saw one solitary specimen. This same story could be repeated from all over Africa, though it must be admitted that the Nile crocodile is by no means the species worst hit by the handbag craze. It may even be said to have fared best so far, for it is not yet in immediate danger of extinction. There still are good numbers in various national parks and reserves, though poaching has become a major problem in some of them. Everything possible should be done to prevent further illicit killing in the Murchison Falls National Park, for the concentration of crocodiles to be seen in the Victoria Nile is unique for East Africa and has become a great tourist attraction. To preserve it is in Uganda's very own interest.

Nothing certain is known regarding the present status of the Long-nosed and Broad-fronted crocodiles. The latter species, rather uncommon, inhabiting small forest streams in remote areas and not much of a prize for a skin-hunter, may have a fairly good chance of survival.

The crocodilians of southern Asia are in much greater danger than the Nile crocodile. The big reptiles are theoretically protected in India, but it has been admitted that owing to the laws on hunting not being enforced, there is a flourishing trade in skins. The situation does not seem to be much better in Pakistan, and this means a grave threat to both the continental mugger and the peculiar and inoffensive gavial. The False gavial has always been a rather rare and local species. In Sarawak, for instance, it was found in any abundance in only one river. Nothing is known of its present status.

Reliable information is also lacking on the Siamese and Philippine crocodiles, but in view of the uncontrolled slaughter of wildlife that is going on in most countries of southern and south-eastern Asia one can only fear the worst. Ceylon appears to make a laudable exception, with crocodiles fully protected by law and the export of skins strictly forbidden. Nobody seems to know for certain whether the Chinese alligator still survives.

In the parts of New Guinea under Australian administration there has been overhunting on a large scale. H. Robert Bustard sums up the situation in the following words:

> Crocodile shooting for profit has been in operation in the Territory for almost twenty years, in the early years almost exclusively by expatriates. Crocodiles were very numerous, large specimens were common, and people admit having shot many more crocodiles than they could possibly skin. The result was a drastic reduction in numbers, especially in the medium size (6–10 ft.) which produces the best quality skins. Skin prices have risen steeply in recent years, so, as the animals became less abundant, shooters turned to smaller crocodiles which provided skins previously unacceptable. The intensified hunting for young crocodiles completely disguised the downward trend of populations.

In two nights on the Fly River, Bustard saw an average of four crocodiles, while in course of eight nights spent on the Sepik only six were observed.

In most of the northern Australian rivers saltwater crocodiles have been practically shot out since the end of World War II. On a trip of nearly five months in 1965, which took him from the Gulf of Carpentaria to the eastern coast of Queensland, Australian animal photographer Graham Pizzey was not able to find even a single specimen. In Western Australia the species has recently been given total protection for a duration of 10 years. Johnston's crocodile has been protected in Western Australia since 1962 and in the Northern Territory since 1964. Queensland, for some obscure reason, saw fit to lag behind and this has led not only to continued slaughter in that state, but to poaching expeditions across the border into the Northern Territory and Western Australia. The remaining populations of the harmless little freshwater crocodile have been rapidly and shamefully depleted in the interests of tourism, which in other parts of the world may yet play a great part in preserving crocodilians. Graham Pizzey reports:

> Of all the indignities suffered by Australian wildlife, the annual fate of thousands of young Johnston's crocodiles in north Queensland, at least until recently, is one of the most unfortunate. Increasing numbers of tourists who come to the north looking for something exotic to take home have

brought about the growth of a destructive industry. Hunters net the more remote rivers and billabongs where young freshwater crocodiles are abundant. The fierce, but timid little creatures are drowned, skinned, mounted in rampant poses, given piercing glass eyes, the insides of their mouths are painted a totally unnatural brilliant scarlet, and the whole ghastly result is clear lacquered. You pay up to 20 Dollars or more for these tasteless objects in gift shops, barber shops, sports stores and so on.

*Freshwater crocodile (Crocodylus johnstoni)*

Pizzey wrote these lines in 1966, and one can only hope that the authorities have since woken up and prohibited the sale of these monstrosities.

The Cuban crocodile is in immediate danger of extinction, and the status of Morelet's crocodile cannot be regarded as much better. There are, however, a few localities where the latter species still occurs and where it could be effectively protected. The American crocodile has been drastically reduced in numbers all through its vast area of distribution. In Florida there is a certain amount of poaching, but by far the worst threat comes from the destruction of nesting sites through real estate development.

The situation in Colombia is described as similar to that encountered in India: crocodiles are legally protected, but nobody bothers to enforce the law. This has resulted in the near-extinction of both the American and the Orinoco crocodiles within the borders of that country.

The Marquis de Wavrin found the crocodilians of the Orinoco basin being rapidly decimated during the 1930s. The first skin-hunters to appear in the area were escaped convicts from Cayenne who went out at night and harpooned the reptiles by the light of torches. A providential slump in the price of skins, which made hunting unremunerative even for convicts on the run, gave the saurians a respite. The slaughter was, however, resumed on a much larger scale after the war. Because of the bony plates underneath their belly skins, caimans had hitherto been regarded as of inferior quality, but shooters now simply took to killing immature specimens of up to about 80 cm in length in which these plates or 'buttons' are not yet developed. Large numbers of young caimans have also been exported to the United States as 'alligators', either alive for the pet trade, or stuffed like the Queensland monstrosities. Spectacled and Black caimans, recorded in such large numbers by Bates, Kerr, Krieg and others, have now become very rare in most areas.

Present-day naturalists would give almost anything for a glimpse of Florida as William Bartram saw it, not as a holiday playground and speculators' paradise but as a magnificent and unspoilt wilderness full of birds and alligators. On the San Juan River Bartram once came upon an enormous mass of fish all pushing through a narrow pass into a small lake. Alligators were taking full advantage of this migration, and from where he stood, the explorer could see them 'in such incredible numbers and so close together from shore to shore, that it would have been easy to have walked across on their heads had the animals been harmless'. That was Florida in the eighteenth century!

Today the American alligator figures on the list of endangered reptiles compiled by the International Union for the Conservation of Nature (IUCN). Alligator skins, being thinner than crocodiles' and more easily processed, have long been in use for making shoes, boots and saddle bags, and it is estimated that approximately 2,500,000 alligators were killed in Florida from 1800 to 1899, and 3,500,000 in Louisiana from 1800 to 1933. The rapid decline throughout the 1930s is well brought out by the fact that in 1929 a total of 190,000 hides were sold in Florida at 70 cents a foot, as compared with a mere 6,800 at 3 dollars a foot in 1943! Since then the price has gone up to 7 or 8 dollars a foot. Alligators have for some time been protected in all states where they used to occur, but the luxury trade prices give the poachers every incentive to take a considerable amount of risks. They could in actual fact count on making such good profits that an occasional fine hardly mattered at all. No wonder that from 1954 to 1968 the species has declined by about 30 per cent in its main stronghold of southern Florida.

I expect that some people on perusing this sad balance sheet will sum up their opinion in the words: 'Good riddance!' The 'hate-the-croc' campaign still goes on, kept alive through the not very factual books by or about skin-hunters, and to create an atmosphere of sympathetic understanding towards the crocodilians is a very difficult task indeed! It certainly is very much easier to rouse public opinion on behalf of elegant egrets and beautiful birds of paradise, of cuddlesome koalas and appealingly big-eyed seal pups. The spotted cats have a very considerable aesthetic appeal, and efforts aimed at saving them from ending up on the backs of gold-digging playgirls and ageing film stars have recently been crowned by some very gratifying successes. But what can be said for the crocodiles? 'Ugly brutes!'—but I have seen the crocodilian grin on quite a number of human faces. 'Loathsome maneaters!'—most species are either quite inoffensive or attack humans only on rare occasions. Some Nile crocodiles and saltwater crocodiles can certainly be dangerous to man, particularly if due caution is not observed, but so can motor cars and planes, and I don't think that we shall get rid of them to save human lives.

Apart from organisms causing epidemic diseases, by far the worst enemy of man is, after all, man himself. Compared with the orgies of mass slaughter instigated so frequently by religious and political maniacs, the toll taken by crocodiles—and by all other wild animals—is not worth talking about. While this marked tendency to control his own numbers by intraspecific predation may give man something in common with the crocodilians, it is he, and not the saurian, who weeps over his victims. One is quite often brought to the shocked realisation that a person can speak emotionally about 'human dignity' and the 'sanctity of human life', while at the same time approving of some of the worst excesses in history and sympathising with what amounts to wholesale murder and robbery. Just think this over for a while, and you will find crocodiles quite harmless and agreeable!

There are, however, plenty of very sound reasons for calling an immediate halt to the uncontrolled slaughter of crocodilians. Whether we like it or not, we have to face the undeniable fact that the skins of these reptiles are at present worth a lot of money. Their export can add quite materially to the national income of a country, but this revenue will vanish like a pricked bubble the moment the reptiles have been exterminated or at least reduced to such a low level that it is no longer worth while to go and look for them. It would, therefore, be a paying proposition to legalise shooting in such a way that breeding stocks are preserved and populations can be cropped without being depleted. Skins would then be available for as long as anybody is ready to pay for them. This should have been obvious right from the beginning of the crocodile-skin boom, but the moral attached to the story of the goose with the golden eggs is something that simply will not enter the average human skull. I hate animals being exploited for the benefit of luxury trades, but if this cannot be stopped, then it should at least only be tolerated under conditions of sound game management. The fur seals of the Pribilof Islands have been saved in this way, and the same can be done with the crocodilians.

Anybody visiting the Murchison Falls National Park cannot fail to realise the tremendous value of crocodiles—alive, not as stuffed monstrosities—to the tourist industry. He may himself not exactly 'like' the saurians he sees—as one likes giraffes and zebras—but he will certainly be thrilled and greatly impressed by them. Most human beings are said to fear and loathe snakes, but snake parks always draw large crowds, and one of the few complaints I have heard from visitors to East Africa has been the apparent absence of these reptiles. Being conditioned to the Tarzan type jungles of the film producers, people are usually disappointed at not having had some agreeably horrifying encounter with them. There is no lack of snakes, but as they are secretive and often nocturnal the tourist spending a fortnight travelling around the country in a car has very little chance of ever seeing one. The average person's attitude to crocodiles runs on similar lines. Together with snakes the big saurians form part and parcel of the jungle atmosphere, and I expect that the sight of the scaly monsters causes many a delightfully primeval shudder. While it is difficult to use snakes as a tourist attraction—except in the form of a snake park— crocodiles, specially where they are present in large numbers, make an excellent spectacle and can be photographed to good advantage. Care must, however, be taken not to approach nesting sites at breeding time. Disturbing the female on guard over her eggs will, as we have seen, lead to quick and devastating raids by monitor lizards and other predators.

There are still good numbers of crocodiles in Lake Rudolf and the Kenya authorities have recently decided to declare the north-eastern part of this large sheet of brackish water—roughly from a point near Allia Bay to Ileret—a national park. The project is receiving the financial support of an American organisation, the Wildlife Leadership Foundation, and crocodiles are sure to become one of the main attractions of this new reserve.

There is no reason why India, Pakistan, Queensland and many South American countries should not have crocodilian attractions to rival these East African national parks.

The important part played by the Nile crocodile in the ecology of African waters has been clearly documented, and the adverse effect its extermination is known to have on fisheries should provide a further incentive to the protection of this species. Similar data are unfortunately not available for other crocodilians—with the exception of the American alligator—and we know nothing whatsoever of their true place in the ecosystems of South American, Asian and Australian rivers.

In view of the materialistic times we live in, the economic value of crocodilians—especially with regard to tourism and the skin trade— is sure to furnish by far the strongest arguments for assuring their survival, though as a naturalist I cannot help thinking that first and foremost they should be preserved for what they really are: not 'hideous monsters' or 'loathsome beasts' but living monuments of almost unbelievable antiquity! The day a hunter kills the last of them, a direct link with the age of the dinosaurs will have been severed.

We humans pride ourselves on having a great regard for everything that is old, a regard that made us spend large sums of money on saving the wonderful temple of Abu Simbel from being submerged by the waters of the Aswan Dam. Stacks of chipped flints and broken pots are jealously hoarded by antiquities departments, officials are appointed to mount guard over ancient monuments. Why can we not extend this perfectly justified regard to the monuments nature has created? Why should the ancient Order of Crocodilians be sacrificed just because bags made from the skins of these animals have become a status symbol? They are monuments, too, mementoes of a past so distant that by comparison even the oldest human artefacts are but of yesterday!

Fortunately, we do not have to close this survey of the world's crocodilians on an entirely sombre note. Efforts are now being made to save the fascinating saurians, and there is some hope that they may be successful.

Rapidly growing concern over the plight of the alligator in a not inconsiderable part of the American public has led to the formation of the American Alligator Council in 1968, and this body of dedicated biologists and conservationists has already made its presence felt. On 5 December 1969, President Nixon signed an endangered species Bill into federal law, prohibiting the interstate shipment of alligators and alligator skins, and this was followed almost immediately by Mayor Lindsay signing a law which, from January 1970 onwards, banned the sale of alligator products in New York City, defaulters being subjected to one year's imprisonment or a 1,000 dollar fine, and confiscation of the merchandise. Those were very important victories for the conservationists, and *Animal Kingdom*, the excellent magazine of the New York Zoological Society, was fully justified in calling 1969 the 'Year of the Alligator'. It could, however, also have been called the 'Year of the Crocodilians', for it saw the establishment of a Crocodile Group within the Survival Service Commission of the IUCN. With the financial support of the World Wildlife Fund it is now possible to collect the data needed in order to give advice on crocodile conservation, and there are encouraging signs that governments and administrators will avail themselves of such services and are willing to listen to what the experts tell them. H. Robert Bustard, for instance, was invited to Australian New Guinea to make a study of both the saltwater and the freshwater crocodile, and to work out ways and means for preserving the two species and bringing their numbers up to an economic level again. He recommended the introduction of a lower size-limit to safeguard small animals until they reach profitable dimensions, and of an upper size-limit to protect the breeding population. This was accepted, and shooting is now restricted to specimens of about 1.80 to 2.10 metres. Bustard's problem was somewhat complicated by the fact that he was dealing with two species of different size and growth rate. Should similar measures be envisaged in eastern and southern Africa, they would have to be tailored for one species only, the Nile crocodile, which reaches sexual maturity when between about 2.40 and 3 metres in length.

If the laws formulated for the preservation of crocodilians are strictly enforced and poachers kept out of national parks and reserves, there is no reason why the depleted populations should not begin to build up again. Recovery can, moreover, be speeded up by the implementation of restocking programmes. An excellent and highly successful hatchery and restocking scheme has in fact been in operation for some time under the sponsorship of the Natal National Parks board, and the status of the Nile crocodile is now probably on a safer basis in Zululand than almost anywhere else.

Eggs are collected from the nests of wild crocodiles and put into incubation boxes, where they are subjected to a temperature of 26.7 to 35°C. With predation completely eliminated, the survival rate of eggs and hatchlings is, of course, very high. The youngsters which hatch after about twelve weeks, are then kept in enclosures until they are big enough to be set free in localities chosen for restocking.

The establishment of a similar hatchery somewhere in India would ensure the survival of the gavial and the mugger. In the Atlanta Zoo in Georgia, USA, an attempt is being made to breed up Morelet's crocodile in captivity, while the Bronx Zoo, which is fortunate enough to own a couple of Chinese alligators, is trying to save this highly endangered species from extinction. The same should be done for the Cuban crocodile.

The so-called 'Alligator Farms' in Florida must be considered as mere show-places where a number of alligators are displayed under rather too crowded conditions. There has been some egg-laying, but the reproduction rate of these captive saurians has never been anywhere near what would be required for proper farming with a continuous renewal of stocks. Experiments in this direction are now being under-taken with Nile crocodiles at the Kajansi Research Station in Uganda.

All is not yet lost for the crocodilians, and I sincerely hope that they will be around to thrill future generations. By then man's regard for his fellow creatures may possibly have progressed to a point where crocodile handbags, snakeskin shoes and leopard coats will generally be considered as symbols of barbarity and bad taste.

# Bibliography

Abel, Othenio. *Lebensbilder aus der Tierwelt der Vorzeit* (Jena 1922)

Adams, Andrew Leith. *Wanderings of a Naturalist in India, the Western Himalayas and Cashmere* (Edinburgh 1867)

Alexander, Boyd. *From the Niger to the Nile* (1907)

Ames, Delano. *Egyptian Mythology* (1965)

Anon. 'The Year of the Alligator', *Animal Kingdom*, LXXII, 6 (1969)

Arnold, Rud. *Das Tier in der Weltgeschichte* (Frankfurt 1939)

Attenborough, David. *Zoo Quest in Madagascar* (1961)

Augusta, Josef & Burian, Zdenek. *Prehistoric Sea Monsters* (1964)

Bakeless, John. *The Eyes of Discovery: The Pageant of North America as seen by the first Explorers* (New York 1961)

Baker, John R. *Man and Animals in the New Hebrides* (1929)

Baker, Samuel White. *The Albert Nyanza, Great Basin of the Nile* (1866)

Baker, Sir Samuel W. *The Nile Tributaries of Abyssinia* (1868)

——*Wild Beasts and their Ways* (1890)

——*The Rifle and Hounds in Ceylon* (1892)

——*Ismailia: A Narrative of the Expedition to Central Africa for the Suppression of the Slave Trade* (1895)

Baldwin, William Charles. *African Hunting and Adventure from Natal to the Zambesi* (1894)

Ball, V. *Jungle Life in India* (1880)

Barker, R. de la Bere. 'Crocodiles', *Tanganyika Notes and Records*, No 34 (1953)

Barrett, Charles. *An Australian Animal Book* (Melbourne 1947)

—— *Wild Life of Australia* (Melbourne, no date)

Bartram, William. *The Travels of William Bartram*, edited by Mark van Doren (New York 1928)

Bary, Erwin de. *Le Dernier Rapport d'un Européen sur Ghat et les Touareg de l'Aïr*, traduit et anoté par Henri Schirmer (Paris 1898)

Bates, Henry Walter. *The Naturalist on the River Amazon* (1892)

Beck, Pierre & Huard, Paul. *Tibesti: carrefour de la préhistoire saharienne* (Paris 1969)

Behrmann, Walter. *Im Stromgebiet des Sepik* (Berlin 1922)

Bellairs, Angus & Carrington, Richard. *The World of Reptiles* (1966)

Belt, Thomas. *A Naturalist in Nicaragua* (1874)

Beltran, Enrique. 'Morelet's Crocodile—Propagation programme in Mexico', *World Wildlife Yearbook* (Morges 1968)

Bentley, W. Holman. *Pioneering on the Congo* (1900)

Bere, Rennie. *Wild Animals in an African National Park* (1966)

Berger, A. *In Afrikas Wildkammern als Forscher und Jaeger* (Berlin 1910)

Berger, Arthur. *So sah ich die Welt* (Berlin 1945)

Besser, Hans. *Natur- und Jagdstudien in Deutsch Ostafrika* (Stuttgart 1917)

Bodenheimer, F. S. *Animal Life in Palestine* (Jerusalem 1935)

Brander, A. A. Dunbar. *Wild Animals in Central India* (1927)

Brazaitis, Peter. 'Endangered!' *Animal Kingdom*, Vol LXX, No 4 (August 1967)

Brehm, Alfred Edmund. *Reiseskizzen aus Nord-Ost-Afrika* (Jena 1862)

——*Tierleben: Allgemeine Kunde des Tierreichs*, 4th edition (Leipzig 1925)

British Museum: *A General Introductory Guide to the Egyptian Collections* (1930)

Brown, C. Barrington. *Canoe and Camp Life in British Guiana* (1877)

Burton, R. G. *Les Mangeurs d'Hommes* (Paris 1932)

Bustard, H. Robert. 'A Future for Crocodiles', *Oryx*, Vol X, No 4 1969

——'Crocodilians of the World—Summary of the Present Position', *World Wildlife Yearbook* (Morges 1969)

Buettikofer, J. *Reisebilder aus Liberia* (Leiden 1890)

Cameron, Verney Lovett. *Across Africa* (1877)

Cansdale, G. S. *Animals and Man* (1952)

——*Reptiles of West Africa* (1955)

Caras, Roger A. *Dangerous to Man. Wild Animals: A definite study of their reputed dangers to Man* (Philadelphia–New York 1964)

Cardinall, A. W. *In Ashanti and Beyond* (1927)

Carpenter, G. D. Hale. *A Naturalist on Lake Victoria* (1920)

Carr, Archie. *The Reptiles* (Life Nature Library 1964)

Champion, F. W. *With a Camera in Tiger-Land* (1928)

Chapman, Abel. *Savage Sudan. Its Wild Tribes, Big-Game and Bird-Life* (1921)

Cheminaud, Guy. *Les Bêtes Sauvages de l'Indochine: Mes Chasses au Laos* (Paris 1939)

Chochod, Louis. *La Faune Indochinoise* (Paris 1950)

Christy, Cuthbert. *Big Game and Pygmies* (1929)

Churchill, Winston Spencer. *My African Journey* (1908)

Clair, Colin. *Unnatural History* (London–New York 1967)

Clarke, James. *Man is the Prey* (1969)

Cloudsley-Thompson, J. L. *The Zoology of Tropical Africa* (1969)

Colbert, Edwin H. *Dinosaurs, their Discovery and their World* (1962)

——*The Age of Reptiles* (1965)

Cott, Hugh B. *Zoological Photography in Practice* (1956)

——*Uganda in Black and White* (1959)

——'Scientific results of an inquiry into the ecology and economic status of the Nile Crocodile (Crocodilus niloticus) in Uganda and Northern Rhodesia', *Transactions of the Zoological Society of London*, Vol 29, Part 4 (1961)

——'Tourists and Crocodiles in Uganda', *Oryx*, Vol X (1969)

Cranworth, Lord. *Profit and Sport in British East Africa* (1919)

Dahl, Knut. *In Savage Australia* (1926)

Dawkins, John. *Rogues and Marauders* (1967)

Decary, Raymond. *La Faune Malgache* (Paris 1950)

Deraniyagala, P. E. P. *Tetrapod Reptiles of Ceylon*, Vol I (Colombo 1967)

Ditmars, Raymond L. *Reptiles of the World* (New York 1967)

Du Chaillu, Paul B. *Explorations and Adventures in Equatorial Africa* (New York 1861)

Dugmore, A. Radclyffe. *Camera Adventures in the African Wilds* (1910)

Dupeyrat, André. *Papua: Beasts and Men* (1963)

Edwards, Amelia R. *A Thousand Miles up the Nile* (1891)

Eisentraut, Martin. *Die Wirbeltiere des Kamerungebirges* (Hamburg–Berlin 1963)

Etchecopar, R. D. & Huë, François. *The Birds of North Africa* (Edinburgh–London 1967)

Finn, Frank. 'Reptilia of India', in Sterndale's *Mammals of India* (1929)

Fonck, Heinrich. *Deutsch Ost-Afrika* (Berlin 1910)

Foran, W. Robert. *A Breath of the Wilds* (1958)

Forsyth, J. *The Highlands of Central India* (1919)

Gee, E. P. *The Wild Life of India* (1964)

Gehrts, M. *A Camera Actress in the Wilds of Togoland* (1915)

Gelfand, Michael. *The African Witch* (Edinburgh–London 1967)

Gibbons, A. St H. *Exploration and Hunting in Central Africa*, 1895–96 (1898)

Gibbons, S. St H. *Africa from South to North through Marotseland* (London–New York 1904)

Goeldi, E. A. *See:* Brehm, 1925

Guggisberg, C. A. W. *Riesentiere und Zwergmenschen* (Berne 1956)
——*Man and Wildlife* (1970)

Guibe, J. 'Les Crocodiles', in *Le Grand Livre de la Faune Africaine et de sa Chasse* (Zurich–Geneva 1954)

Guppy, Nicholas. *Wai-Wai: Through the Forests north of the Amazon* (1958)

Gurney, J. H. *Rambles of a Naturalist in Egypt and other Countries* (1876)

Hauff, Bernhard. *Das Holzmadenbuch* (Oehringen 1960)

Hellmich, Walter. 'Herpetologische Ergebnisse einer Forschungsreise nach Angola', *Veroeffentlichungen der Zoologischen Staatssammlung Muenchen*, Vol 5 (1957)

Herodot: *Reisen und Forschungen in Afrika*, edited by Dr H. Treidler (Leipzig 1926)

Heuglin, M. Th von. *Ornithologie Nordost-Afrika's* (Cassel 1869)

Hickson, Sydney A. *A Naturalist in North Celebes* (1889)

Hoier, R. *A travers Plaines et Volcans au Parc National Albert* (Brussels 1950)

Honegger, René E. 'Alligatoren-Farmen existieren nicht!' *Aquaria*, 16, 7 (St Gallen)
——Beobachtungen an der Herpetofauna der Seychellen. *Salamandra* Bd. 1/2, 1966

Hornaday, William T. *Two Years in the Jungle: The Experiences of a Hunter and Naturalist in India, Ceylon, the Malay Peninsula and Borneo* (1885)
——*A Wild Animal Roundup* (New York–London 1925)
——*American Natural History*, 14th edition (New York–London 1927)

Hose, Charles. *Fifty Years of Romance and Research, or A Jungle-Wallah at Large* (1927)

Howells, Victor. *A Naturalist in Palestine* (1956)

Humboldt, Alexander von. *Personal Narrative of Travels to the Equinoctial Regions of America* (1852)

Hunter, J. A. *White Hunter* (No Date)

Hvass, Hans. *Reptiles and Amphibians of the World* (1958)

Jennison, George. *Animals for Show and Pleasure in Ancient Rome* (Manchester 1937)

Johnson, Walford B. 'Crocodiles and other Reptiles', in *Wild Life Illustrated* (No date)

Johnston, H. H. *The River Congo, from its Mouth to Bolobo* (1884)

Johnston, Sir Harry H. *British Central Africa* (1897)

——*The Uganda Protectorate* (1902)

Joset, P. E. *Les Sociétés secrètes des Hommes-Léopards en Afrique Noire* (Paris 1955)

Kearton, Cherry, and Barnes, James. *Through Central Africa from East to West* (1915)

Kearton, Cherry. *In the Land of the Lion* (1929)

——*Adventures with Animals and Men* (1936)

Keller, C. *Madagascar, Mauritius and the other East-African Islands* (1901)

Kerr, Sir John Graham. *A Naturalist in the Gran Chaco* (Cambridge 1950)

King, Wayne. 'American Alligator, Alligator mississipiensis', *Animal Kingdom*, LXXII, 6 (1969)

Kingsley, Mary H. *Travels in West Africa*, 3rd edition (1956)

Koch-Isenburg, Ludwig. *Urwelt im Aufbruch: Ein Tierfreund erlebt Madagaskar* (Frankfurt 1961)

Krieg, Hans. *Zwischen Anden und Atlantik* (Munich 1948)

Kruger National Park: 'Annual Report of the Biologist, 1958/1959', *Koedoe*, No 3 (1960)

Kuehlmann, D. A. 'Putzerfische saeubern Krokodile (Crocodylus acutus)', *Zeitsch. f. Tierpsychologie*, 23, 7 .

Kuhn, Oskar. *Lurche und Kriechtiere der Vorzeit* (Stuttgart 1958)

——*Die Tierwelt des Solnhofer Schiefers* (Stuttgart 1966)

Kuhnert, Wilhelm. *Im Lande meiner Modelle* (Leipzig 1923)

Lhote, Henri. *La Chasse chez les Touaregs* (Paris 1951)

Livingstone, David. *Narrative of an Expedition to the Zambesi and its tributaries and the discovery of the lakes Shirwa and Nyassa* (1865)

——*The Zambezi Expedition of David Livingstone*, 1858–1863, edited by J. P. Wallis (1956)

——*Livingstone's Private Journals* 1851–1853, edited with an Introduction by I. Schapera (1960)

Loveridge, Arthur. 'Check List of the Reptiles and Amphibians of

East Africa (Uganda; Kenya; Tanganyika; Zanzibar)', *Bull Mus Comp Zoology*, Harvard College, Vol 117, No 2 (Cambridge, Mass, 1957)

Mackenzie, D. R. *The Spirit-ridden Konde* (1925)

McIlhenny, E. A. *The Alligator's Life History* (Boston 1935)

Maugham, R. C. F. *Wild Game in Zambesia* (1914)

Meinertzhagen, R. *Pirates and Predators* (Edinburgh–London 1959)

Mertens, Robert. *Quer durch Australien* (Frankfurt 1958)

——*The World of Amphibians and Reptiles* (1960)

——'Putzer-Voegel bei Krokodilen', *Natur und Museum*, 98, 5 (1968)

Miller, Leo E. *In the Wilds of South America* (New York 1919)

Mjoeberg, Eric. *In der Wildnis des tropischen Urwaldes. Abenteuer und Schilderungen aus Niederlaendisch Indien* (Leipzig 1930)

Moffett, J. P. (editor). *Handbook of Tanganyika*, 2nd edition (Dar es Salaam 1958)

Monkman, Noel. *Escape to Adventure* (Sydney 1956)

Monod, Théodore. 'Die Fauna der Sahara', in Christoph Krueger. *Sahara* (Vienna–Munich 1967)

Monteiro, Joachim John. *Angola and the River Congo* (1875)

Mountford, Guy. *The Vanishing Jungle. Two Wildlife Expeditions to Pakistan* (1969)

Neubert, Otto. *The Valley of the Kings* (1957)

Neumann, Arthur H. *Elephant-Hunting in East Equatorial Africa* (1898)

Owen, T. R. H. *Hunting Big Game with Gun and Camera* (1960)

Parrinder, Geoffrey. *African Mythology* (1967)

Percival, A. Blainey. *A Game Ranger on Safari* (1928)

Petersen, Kai. *Prehistoric Life on Earth* (1963)

Pitman, C. R. S. *A Game Warden among his Charges* (1931)

——*A Game Warden takes Stock* (1945)

——'The Cold-blooded Creatures (Reptiles and Amphibians)', in *Uganda National Parks' Handbook* (Kampala 1962)

Pizzey, Graham. *Animals and Birds in Australia* (Melbourne 1966)

Poignant, Roslyn. *Oceanic Mythology* (1967)

Pooley, A. C. 'Preliminary Studies on the Breeding of the Nile Crocodile, *Crocodylus niloticus*, in Zululand', *Lammergeyer*, No 10 (1969)

——'Some Observations on the rearing of Crocodiles', *Lammergeyer*, No 10 (1969)

——'The Burrowing Behaviour of Crocodiles', *Lammergeyer*, No 10 (1969)

Pope, Clifford H. 'Collecting in Northern and Central China', in *The New Conquest of Central Asia*, Vol I. The American Museum of Natural History (New York 1932)

——*The Reptile World* (1956)

Powell-Cotton, P. H. G. *In Unknown Africa* (1904)

Regan, Charles Tate. *Natural History* (1946)

Rittlinger, Herbert. *Ethiopian Adventure* (1959)

Romer, Alfred Sherwood. *Vergleichende Anatomie der Wirbeltiere* (Hamburg–Berlin 1959)

——*The Procession of Life* (1968)

Roosevelt, Theodore. *African Game Trails* (New York 1910)

——*Through the Brazilian Wilderness* (1914)

Rose, Walter. *The Reptiles and Amphibians of Southern Africa* (Cape Town 1950)

Roure, Georges, *Faune et Chasse en Afrique Occidentale Française* (Dakar 1956)

St John, J. A. *Egypt and Nubia.* (London, no date)

Sanderson, G. P. *Thirteen Years among the Wild Beasts of India*, 7th edition (Edinburgh 1912)

Schmidt, Karl. P. & Inger, Robert F. *Living Reptiles of the World* (1957)

Schomburgk, Hans. *Fahrten und Forschungen mit Buechse und Film im unbekannten Africa* (Berlin 1928)

Schomburgk, Robert. *See:* Brehm, 1925

Schweinfurth, Georg. *The Heart of Africa* (1878)

Selous, Frederick Courtney. *A Hunter's Wanderings in Africa* (1890)

——*Travel and Adventure in South-East Africa* (1893)

——*African Nature Notes and Reminiscences* (1908)

Seurat, L. G. *Exploration Zoologique de l'Algérie, de 1830 à 1930* (Paris 1930)

Severy, Merle. *America's Wonderland: The National Parks and Monuments of the United States* (Washington 1959)

Shelford, Robert W. C. *A Naturalist in Borneo* (1916)

Sibree, James. *A Naturalist in Madagascar* (1915)

Sick, Helmut. *Tukani* (Hamburg–Berlin 1957)

Smith, Andrew. *The Diary of Dr. Andrew Smith, Director of the*

"*Expedition for Exploring Central Africa*" *1834–1836*, edited by Percival R. Kerby (Cape Town 1939–40)

Smith, T. Murray. *The Nature of the Beast* (1963)

Smolik, Hans- Wilhelm. *Rororo Tierlexikon*, Bd 4, 'Kriechtiere, Lurche, Fische' (Guetersloh 1969)

Smythies, Bertrand E. *The Birds of Borneo* (Edinburgh–London 1960)

Sonnini, C. S. *Travels in upper and lower Egypt* (1799)

Spatz, Paul. 'Wie und wo ich das sagenhafte Saharakrokodil fand', *Kosmos*, 27, 6 (1930)

Stanley, Henry M. *Through the Dark Continent* (1878)

Stevenson-Hamilton, J. *Animal Life in Africa* (1912)

——*Wild Life in South Africa* (1954)

Swinnerton, H. H. *Outlines of Palaeontology* (1949)

——*Fossils* (1960)

Swinton, W. E. *Fossil Amphibians and Reptiles*, British Museum—Natural History (1958)

——*The Dinosaurs* (1970)

Sykes, C. A. *Service and Sport on the Tropical Nile* (1903)

Temple-Perkins, E. A. *Kingdom of the Elephant* (1955)

Thomas, H. B. & Scott, Robert. *Uganda* (1949)

Tornier, Gustav. 'Reptilien und Amphibien Kriechthiere', in *Deutsch-Ost-Africa*, Bd III (Berlin 1895)

Tweedie, M. W. F. & Harrison, J. L. *Malayan Animal Life* (London–Kuala Lumpur 1965)

Vareschi, Volkmar. *Geschichtslose Ufer: Auf den Spuren Humboldts am Orinoko* (Munich 1959)

Vinton, Kenneth W. *The Jungle Whispers* (1956)

Vogel, Zdenek. *Reptile Life* (No date)

Wake, D. B. & Kluge, A. G. 'The Machris Expedition to Tschad', *Africa Contr Sci Los Angeles County Mus*, 40 (1961)

Waterton, Charles. *Wanderings in South America*, edited with biographical Introduction and Explanatory Index by the Rev J. G. Wood (1880)

Wavrin, Marquis de. *Les Bêtes Sauvages de l'Amazonie* (Paris 1939)

Wermuth, H. & Mertens, R. *Schildkroeten-Krokodile-Brueckenechsen* (Jena 1961)

Wethered, H. N. *The Mind of the Ancient World: A Consideration of Pliny's Natural History* (1937)

Willock, Colin. *The enormous Zoo; A Profile of the Uganda National Parks* (1964)

Worthington, S. & E. B. *Inland Waters of Africa* (1933)

Zwilling, Ernst A. *Unvergessenes Kamerun* (Berlin 1939)

# Index